DIY
Rustic Modern
METAL CRAFTS

DIY Rustic Modern METAL CRAFTS

35 Creative Upcycling Ideas for Galvanized Metal

LAURA PUTNAM

of Finding Home, findinghomefarms.com

adamsmedia

Avon, Massachusetts

Published by
Adams Media, a division of F+W Media, Inc.
57 Littlefield Street, Avon, MA 02322. U.S.A.
www.adamsmedia.com

ISBN 10: 1-4405-9134-2
ISBN 13: 978-1-4405-9134-1
eISBN 10: 1-4405-9135-0
eISBN 13: 978-1-4405-9135-8

Printed in the United States of America.

10 9 8 7 6 5 4 3 2 1

Many of the designations used by manufacturers and sellers to distinguish their products are claimed as trademarks. Where those designations appear in this book and F+W Media, Inc. was aware of a trademark claim, the designations have been printed with initial capital letters.

Readers are urged to take all appropriate precautions before undertaking any how-to task. Always read and follow instructions and safety warnings for all tools and materials, and call in a professional if the task stretches your abilities too far. Although every effort has been made to provide the best possible information in this book, neither the publisher nor the author are responsible for accidents, injuries, or damage incurred as a result of tasks undertaken by readers. This book is not a substitute for professional services.

Cover design by Sylvia McArdle.
Photos by Laura Putnam.

This book is available at quantity discounts for bulk purchases.
For information, please call 1-800-289-0963.

DEDICATION

To my DIY partner in crime, the best projects I have ever done have always been the ones with you. Dana, thank you for believing in me always and being the best partner in life I could ask for.

And to our greatest accomplishment—our amazing daughters—thank you for inspiring me each and every day to be more, learn more, and love more.

To my blog readers, I thank you from the bottom of my heart for giving me a place to share my creativity and my heart. I thank you for showing up in this weird world of blogging and encouraging me. *You* are the reason this book has been written and published.

ACKNOWLEDGMENTS

I have reached the end of the journey of writing this book and I am filled with appreciation and gratitude. I had no idea what to expect in this process and I am so thankful for all that I have learned and all that this journey has provided. I never expected to write a book and enjoyed figuring out that this topic, thirty-five galvanized projects for your home, was such a good fit.

I would like to thank Adams Media for this opportunity. I would like to thank my editor, Jacqueline Musser, for believing in me and guiding me through this whole process. Thank you for that e-mail that led to this end result, Jackie!

Thank you, Katie Corcoran Lytle, for guiding me through the edits and making this book the best it could be.

I cannot end this book without sharing what I am most thankful for: my blog readers. From the days when there were just a few of you to today, each and every comment and word of encouragement has warmed my heart. I am so thankful to have this forum and this world of blogging and I thank for you making it possible.

To the friends I am blessed to have in my life, thank you for making life so much better each and every day. Thank you for the laughter that makes it all worthwhile.

To my parents who never discouraged me when I headed down unexpected and nontraditional roads, for cheering me and loving me. I love you all dearly.

Mom, thank you for all of the Friday nights growing up when you sat me on the counter and taught me to believe in myself.

To the Putnam family, thank you for always surprising me with how many times you read my blog and for sending words of encouragement and humor. Pat and Paul, I am truly blessed to count you among my parents.

To my sister, or should I say Sista! Thank you for being my biggest fan, my biggest cheerleader, and for always knowing when I needed to be picked up. I love you beyond words, Lisa, and thank you for loving me right back.

To my Sunshine, your nickname suits you so very perfectly. You are the brightness in each of my days and your humor and unabashed love for life inspire me every day. I love watching how life unfolds for you each and every day. I love you.

To my Peanut, I marvel daily at how you open your kind heart and faith. I learn so much from you and the way you look at the world. I love you.

Last but so far from least, Dana, thank you. You are my rock, you are my best friend and the best partner in life and business I could have ever dreamed of. You make this life so much more interesting and enjoyable. You are the greatest father I have ever known and the greatest business partner I could have dreamed of. Always and forever, no matter what.

PREFACE

I think the seed to be a DIYer was planted early. As a child, I was always in our basement painting, cutting, or coloring something. I still remember my sister helping me create a little art nook with my easel and some towels to create a wall so that I had a special little corner to create in. I worked on a paint-by-number project in that little corner for a long time and then gave it to my grandparents for Christmas. The first time I visited their new home, I saw my painting framed and hung on the wall in their kitchen. I still remember that moment like it was yesterday, of seeing something I created on their wall.

When I was in high school, I remember one fall sitting down and deciding to make all of my Christmas presents for friends and family. I covered photo albums and boxes in fabric and added trim and ribbon. I made myself one of those boxes that year and I still have it filled with cards and notes from my childhood. It still makes me smile when I look at it.

I know now that being a "maker" was just part of who I was, but I just was not aware of it. I am not a talented painter and I couldn't draw my way out of a box, so I decided I wasn't "creative." The maker in me kept trying to come out and would tug at me, but I kept pushing it down. Slowly, I began to realize that I could be creative in ways other than the textbook versions. I found that decorating my home and the homes of friends and family was a new way I could be creative. I started a decorating business and years later I started a blog, *Finding Home*. I was learning to accept a new version of what it means to be creative, but in my mind, I still was not a DIYer. That was for the more talented and creative people.

They say necessity is the greatest form of invention, and my journey to becoming a DIYer started with a deadline. With a deadline looming, my husband and I started out to make a project—in fact, it was the first version of the Three-Tiered Outdoor Planter featured in Chapter 5 of this book. One project led to another, and before we knew it, we were comfortable with taking on DIY projects.

And one day I realized I was a DIYer.

And guess what?

So are you!

I've been lucky enough to turn my love of DIY into something much bigger. And, in much the same way that I never thought of myself as a DIYer just because I like crafting, when I began writing a blog, I never expected to become a "blogger." It has always been, and will likely always be, such a strange concept to me. I really wanted to just hold myself accountable for a handful of goals I had set for myself in my decorating business. Over time, I found I loved the interaction with readers and the push to be creative on a weekly basis. When I look back now, I am amazed at how much I have learned by pushing myself. It truly seems like just yesterday I almost gave up on blogging because I could not figure out how to correctly upload pictures.

Today, my blog has become our family business. We have branched out the Finding Home brand to our handcrafted maple syrup and specialty food line. We have an online store, a wholesale line for retailers, and now a book. You never know the journey life is going to take you on. When I first started my blog, the tag line read, "The stories of the journey we are on to Finding Home." What a beautiful journey it has been so far.

INTRODUCTION

My favorite color is galvanized. Truly, there is something about the texture and the color that makes me weak in the knees. From a bright and shiny new piece to an old vintage piece dug out of a dark corner of a yard sale, I have been filling my home with galvanized accents for years. Every piece has a story; whether it is where it came from or what I did with it when I found it, galvanized accents are one of the things that make my home unique. And, although my home is decorated and styled in a blend of traditional and farmhouse styles, I believe you can use galvanized accents in your home, too—no matter the style.

So what does *galvanized* mean? Galvanized materials are simply iron or steel items that have been coated in a layer of zinc. The zinc is meant to protect the metal and allows it to withstand the elements better. The terms *zinc* and *galvanized* are often used interchangeably when referring to things like a bucket. Throughout the book, you'll find more than thirty different ways you can create projects for your home using galvanized materials, ranging from wall art to lighting to storage and more. The projects cover ideas for many rooms in your home as well as outdoor spaces. The level of difficulty ranges from simply gluing two things together in a creative manner to building a piece of furniture; however, every project is doable for even the most beginner DIYer, so don't worry! Just because a project is labeled "DIY" doesn't mean it has to be complicated. DIY just means looking at materials and ideas in a new way—your way—and making something that personalizes your home.

I am excited for you to try these projects and put your own spin on them. Don't get caught up in thinking you have to make everything perfect or just as you see it in the picture. Use your own ideas, make it better, make it more personal, and enjoy the heck out of it. Just by the fact that you are reading this page, the seed has already been planted in you to be a "maker." It doesn't matter if you are sitting in a full-blown workshop with every tool you could dream of owning or you are sitting at your kitchen table with a tube of glue and a plan—you are a DIYer.

You'll find a chapter in the book that gives you all the information you need on the tools and materials that you will need for these projects as well as the best resources and tips for finding galvanized metal materials, so whatever you want to try, you'll be ready. Try one project in this book or try them all. Do it exactly as I did it, or just be inspired by the idea and create your own version.

This book is a tool to help you and inspire you to try some new projects. Once you realize what you are capable of, your whole outlook changes. You will see something you like in the stores and tell yourself you can make it yourself. You will search and search in the stores and not find what you want, so you will make it yourself. An idea will grow in your head; sometimes it will sit for days and sometimes for months. Eventually, through trial and error, you will figure out how the heck to do it and it will be one of your favorite projects ever . . . until the next one.

Chapter 1
MATERIALS YOU WILL NEED

Nothing is worse than starting a project and not having all of the materials and tools you need to complete it. This chapter provides you with all the information you need to make sure that doesn't happen. Your first step is going to be finding your galvanized materials. Here, I walk you through deciding if you want the rustic patina of vintage pieces, the shiny newness of a store-bought piece, or the tricks needed to make a new piece look old. I also share my best suggestions for finding galvanized materials and pieces, both old and new. One thing to keep in mind when planning out your projects is that you don't need to use exactly the same materials specified in the projects. You can be inspired by what I use and then create your own version.

When you are ready to get started, this chapter also lets you know the tools and craft materials you will need to complete the projects. From the basics of safety materials to the few power tools you will need, and everything in between, I want to make sure missing materials never slow you down on a project. I also share the best places to find your craft materials. Most of the tools used are basics in a toolbox, but there a few useful power tools that make a project easier. Whenever possible, however, I included a nonpowered alternative.

VINTAGE VERSUS NEW

The first thing you need to think about when starting one of these rustic metal crafts is what type of galvanized piece you want to work with: vintage or new. A vintage piece is going to be a unique option that may be one-of-a-kind and have a beautiful patina, while a new piece is going to be easier to find and have a nice shine to it. Truth be told, my first choice is to find the perfect vintage galvanized piece to work with. I love the patina, and I love the story behind each piece. However, it can be hard to find just the right size and piece to work with; many times the best option is to start with a new item.

That said, for each project, the type of finish to use is completely a personal choice. You can choose to use a new item with its store-bought finish, use one of the three aging techniques covered later in this chapter to make the finish look older, or use a vintage item. I have included a mix of all three options within the projects in the book.

WHERE TO FIND VINTAGE GALVANIZED MATERIALS

Shopping for vintage galvanized elements may not be as quick as finding new ones, but in my opinion it can be the most fun. It is like a treasure hunt. Some of my best finds have been at yard sales or at estate sales. I tend to head right to the garage or basement at an estate sale for the best finds, and that is usually where you will find anything galvanized. From time to time, I find galvanized treasures at an auction, but they tend to be a little more expensive that way. Vintage shops are also another option, but you have to watch for over-priced items. When you're looking for vintage materials in these places, you have to look at things with an open eye because they may be dirty or placed in a section with automotive parts that you might not normally dig through.

In addition to these options, take a look online. I have had my best luck on Etsy (*www.etsy.com*) but have also found pieces on eBay (*www.ebay.com*). Just put in the search term "galvanized" and then select the filter for "vintage." Many of the listings on both sites are very expensive, but as you scroll through you will find reasonably priced options from time to time. You have to search through carefully as sellers will sometimes list a reproduction item as a vintage item. You can get a good idea about whether a piece is a reproduction or not by checking to see if the wear marks are a little too perfect looking and if the seller has listed multiples of identical items. Once you find an item you like, click on the seller. If the seller has one galvanized item that is reasonably priced, she will likely have another and will often give you a discount on shipping if you buy multiple items.

WHERE TO FIND NEW GALVANIZED MATERIALS

I have spent a long time hunting through all types of stores to find the best galvanized materials sources, and in the following sections, you'll learn everything I have discovered about finding the best new galvanized materials available. For the projects in this book, your new galvanized materials fall into the following categories:

⊙ sheet metal

⊙ buckets/bins/tubs of varying sizes

⊙ feeding vessels

⊙ strap iron

⊙ stove end caps

⊙ decorative elements (like the letters in the Rustic Letter Sign project in Chapter 2)

Let's take a closer look . . .

Sheet Metal

Sheet metal is best found in the larger hardware stores. Look for varying sizes to get the best fit for a project so you can avoid metal cuts whenever possible. The largest sheets I worked with are 24" × 36" and can be found in the plumbing section. They are packaged in a flat box and can sometimes be challenging to find, but trust me, they are there. You will also find a few sections, like in the hardware aisles, where they have sheet metal displayed in smaller sizes like 12" × 24" along with other types of metal products. I have yet to find a hardware store that will cut metal for you, so for most projects I worked with metal sizes that could be purchased already cut to size.

Buckets/Bins/Tubs

It is getting easier and easier to find options in this category. For your larger tubs, the best bet is to check out the larger hardware stores and feed-supply stores. For the smaller sizes and items of unique shapes and sizes, larger craft stores have a lot of options.

Feeding Vessels

Galvanized feeding pans, feed scoops, and chicken feeders are best found online or in feed-supply stores. In this book, I have used them to make a clock and a mirror, but they work beautifully as trays as well.

Strap Iron

Strap iron is my new favorite galvanized friend. I originally found it at a feed-supply store, but it can also easily be found at large and independent hardware stores. The bendable aspect allows it to trim out endless projects to add a galvanized detail.

Stove End Caps

I have always found the best selection of stove end caps at my local independent hardware store. You can find some in the large hardware stores and online as well. The primary use of stove end caps is to close out the end of stove piping. They come in multiple sizes to accommodate different size pipes and are round, so they are versatile pieces that can be used for planting, making candles, and other decorative projects.

Decorative Elements

Galvanized decorative elements are becoming more and more available both in stores and online. I have found the larger craft stores to offer the best selection and options. From galvanized letters for making signs to buckets from the smallest to the largest, larger craft stores will have the materials you need for many of the projects included in this book.

HOW TO MAKE NEW GALVANIZED METAL LOOK OLD

Do not be discouraged if you can't find the perfect vintage piece you want for these projects. You don't have to give up on that vintage look that you love. Here, I share three ways to make brand new pieces look like they have been passed down for generations. With all three methods, there are a few things to be aware of. First, by the process of what you are doing, you are removing the protective coating. In doing so, this can lead to rust or additional wear over time. Second, every single piece you work with, even if you use the same technique, will respond differently. The key to the aging process (no matter how you go about it) is to be okay with it being a little imperfect and different each time. Third, you need to check the items regularly. Some items will have an immediate response to a technique; others will take a full day to respond. It is important to keep checking because if you let whichever process you are using go too long, you may not like the results and you may end up with rust.

Method One: Mother Nature

This option is by far the easiest. It doesn't use any chemicals, but it does take the longest amount of time to work. Simply leave your new galvanized piece outdoors uncovered. I have had some pieces react to the elements in just a few weeks and others take a few seasons. As with all of these options, each piece will react differently, so it is best to keep checking on it regularly.

For example, some of the best patinas I have ever achieved on galvanized metal has been on planters I left outdoors through a few seasons. I have a galvanized top bench that is outdoors, but covered. It is slowly changing because it is not exposed to rain. I may decide to speed up the aging process and set it out where it is not covered for a few weeks. The benefit of this technique is that it is like getting a whole new piece each month as the age on the metal changes.

Method Two: Vinegar

I am beginning to wonder if there is anything that white vinegar cannot do. Not only does it clean windows and stainless steel, but if left on for several hours, it removes the zinc coating and ages galvanized metal. This method is great because it doesn't use harsh chemicals and works pretty quickly. In fact, I found that the finish darkens quite a bit more than the other methods.

If an item is small, just submerge it in a bucket filled with vinegar. For larger items, like a bucket, soak a rag in vinegar and lay it over the top of the piece. With this method it is important to keep checking on the materials. For some pieces, the vinegar can start to take effect

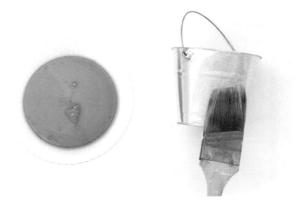

Bucket treated with vinegar (left-hand side) versus bucket treated with toilet bowl cleaner (right-hand side)

almost immediately. For others, it could take several hours to overnight. If your rag dries out before you reach the finish that you want, just add more vinegar. Once you have achieved the aged look that you want, use water to rinse off the metal, and let it dry before crafting.

Method Three: Toilet Bowl Cleaner

The method I have used the most to age new galvanized metal has been this one, which uses toilet bowl cleaner to create a patina. This method is very effective because of the thicker nature of the cleaner and its ability to cling to the side of an item, which helps it effectively remove the item's protective coating. Even though I am not a big fan of using chemicals, especially with the mess and disposal needs of cleanup, I really like the results of this method.

To use this method, make sure you work in an area that is well ventilated, then set up a disposable surface under your work area. I usually use a garbage bag. Simply apply the cleaner to your galvanized metal with a paintbrush and check on it periodically until you get the look you desire. A good guide is to check on your piece after about 15 minutes to see how it is reacting. Then, check on it hourly. I have found most pieces respond anywhere between 30 minutes and 8 hours. Once you have the level of effect on the finish and coloring that you want, use water to rinse off the metal, and let it dry before crafting.

COMMONLY USED TOOLS AND SUPPLIES

Now that you've found your galvanized materials and have them in the finish you want, it's time to get your tools together. One of my favorite parts of the projects chosen for this book is the simplicity of tools needed, as you can see in the following sections. For quite a few projects, you need nothing more than glue. For a few projects, you need some easy-to-use power tools. However, for the majority of the projects, you really just need some metal snips, which are like scissors and are designed specifically for cutting metal, and a drill or screw gun. I wanted to keep things simple and doable for everyone. I know my favorite projects are often ones that are the easiest to do.

Work Gloves, Rubber Gloves, and Eye Protection

Out of all the materials you need to have on hand, these items are the most important and should not be forgotten. Any time you are cutting, drilling, or sawing, you must wear hand protection and eye protection. Any time you are cutting or filing metal, you should wear work gloves and eye protection. When painting or staining, it is always a good idea to wear rubber gloves to avoid covering your hands in stain or paint.

Ruler, Tape Measure, Straightedge, Level, and Framing Square

These items are all designed to make sure your cuts and edges are straight and your materials are the correct size. A ruler, tape measure, and straightedge will help you measure. A straightedge can be a ruler, an oversized ruler, a level, or basically anything with a confirmed straight side to line up points on your projects. A framing square keeps your corners and angles at 90 degrees when you need them to be. A level is designed to measure when you have an item straight.

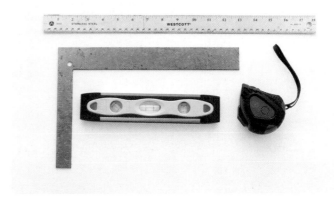

Miter Box, Chop Saw, and Jigsaw

For most of the projects, when wood cuts are needed, a miter box will get the job done. A miter box is simply a plastic box with a saw that fits into slots. The slots ensure you are cutting a perfectly straight line or an angled cut. A miter box means that you don't need a power tool, but it is a bit rough on the hands and arms because of the sawing motion. If you have access to a chop saw, which is just a powered saw that allows you to cut both straight and angled cuts through wood (sometimes called a cut-off saw or miter saw) and are comfortable with safely using it, I say go for it.

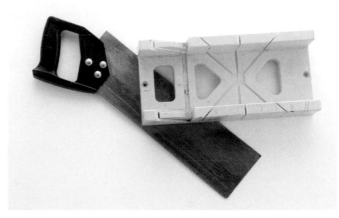

Miter box (bottom)

One project, the Bar Cart (see Chapter 6), uses wood that is too wide for a miter box. That is when you will need to use a chop saw or have your wood cut by a hardware store. Only use a chop saw if you are comfortable and know how to safely use it.

The Advent Tree (see Chapter 7) requires a long cut on an angle, and your best tool for making that cut is a jigsaw. Simply set your wood in place on a work surface that allows the end you are working on to hang off, such as a workbench or a pair of saw horses, hold your jigsaw firmly, pull the trigger, and begin moving along the line you need to cut.

Metal Snips

Often referred to as tin snips, metal snips come in many shapes and sizes, and they are also designed for right-handed and left-handed use. They are designed specifically for cutting metal. For the type of metal cuts needed for the projects in this book, I found a small pair without an angled blade worked best and allowed my hand to have the most control over my cuts. However, for larger cuts like on the Vintage Window Memo Board (see Chapter 2), a larger style may work better for you.

Metal Files

A metal file is an essential tool when any cuts are made in metal. Made of metal itself, it has different levels of grooves on the sides that work as a file to smooth cut and rough edges. Once a cut is made, no matter what type of metals snips you use, you'll need to follow up that cut by filing the edges of the cut metal to remove any burrs and smooth any sharp edges.

Self-Drilling Wood Screws and Sheet Metal Screws

Whenever possible, I've used self-drilling wood screws in the projects throughout the book. These work best with smaller pieces of wood and eliminate the need for drilling a pilot hole. However, whenever there is a need to drill directly into metal, even if there is wood on the other side, I use sheet metal screws because the first surface they need to pull through is metal, and sheet metal screws work best in this scenario.

Drill, Screw Gun, and Hole Saw

Whenever I use the self-drilling wood screws and sheet metal screws, I use a screw gun to attach them. A screw gun is lighter and more comfortable in my hand than a cordless drill, so it is easier to move and less tiring. I use a separate drill for drilling any pilot holes but then actually attach screws with my screw gun. You can use just a drill and change out the bits, but I prefer to switch tools.

There are several projects where you need to create a larger hole than what a drill bit would provide. In these cases, I used a hole saw attachment for my drill to make a larger hole. Hole saws come in many different sizes and should be selected based on the needs of your project.

Crafting Materials

A host of crafting materials are used throughout the projects in this book, including paintbrushes, paint, pencils, permanent markers, wood stain, scissors, and painter's tape. But while these will all come in handy, the most commonly used craft material is glue. Work with a glue that is heavy duty, quick drying, and works with metal. The glue I use is an all-purpose glue that is clear and specifically says it is usable for metal and wood.

So now that we've covered all of the basics like where to buy your materials; how to decide if you are working with new, vintage, or made-to-look-like-vintage materials; and what kinds of tools and supplies you will need, you are ready to get started. I hope you find many projects you want to try and put your own spin on each of them!

Chapter 2
RUSTIC METAL WALL ART

Nothing defines a room more than what you put on your walls. From family pictures to paintings to vintage finds, wall art sets the tone for a room. However, sometimes finding just the right piece in just the right size can be a problem. If you happen to find the right style, sometimes the size just won't work. Or, if you happen to find the right size, the style just doesn't work. By creating your own wall art, you have the opportunity to make what you want in your own style and in the perfect size. And the best part is that no one else will have anything like it! In this chapter you'll learn how to make a series of different projects for your walls like a customized sign, a memo board made out of a repurposed window, a unique mirror, a simple-styled clock, and a display shelf.

New York
[NY]

to love

to seek

New Hampshire
[NH]

VINTAGE WINDOW MEMO BOARD

Memo boards are perfect for keeping track of schedules, phone numbers, photos, and mementos. A memo board basically serves as a spot where you keep things in place, but why not make yours a little more interesting than that? This metal memo board starts with something old—a vintage window—and pairs it with something new—a piece of sheet metal. The combination of the two creates a unique piece of wall art that still functions as a memo board. And, if you want the metal on your memo board to look old, just use the aging techniques shared in Chapter 1 and add even more character to your walls. ▸

Materials

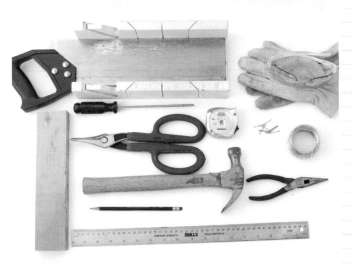

- Vintage window (the one I used measures out at 20" × 36")
- Work gloves
- Eye protection
- 1 heavy-duty trash bag (optional)
- Hammer
- Flat-head screwdriver
- Needle-nose pliers
- Tape measure
- Straightedge
- Pencil

- 24" × 36" piece of sheet metal
- Metal snips
- Miter box
- 4 thin wood strips or pieces of lathe at least as long as your window is wide (The window I used was 36" in width, but size yours according to the window you are using. Lathe come in 48"× 1½"× .31".)
- About 20 (3/4") carpentry nails
- Picture-hanging hardware

1. If your window has glass, begin by wearing your work gloves and eye protection. Then place your window in a heavy-duty trash bag and break out the glass with a hammer. Next, use your screwdriver and pliers to remove all of the remaining glass pieces from the frame. You can use your hammer to tap the end of your screwdriver into the grooves where the glass was held. Keep maneuvering your screwdriver to drive the glass out of the grooves. Pieces that are difficult to remove can be pulled with pliers.

2. Measure the dimensions of the window opening from the back side with your tape measure. Use your straightedge and pencil and transfer those measurements to your metal, and mark your cut line on the back side of the sheet metal. Wear your work gloves and use your metal snips to carefully cut your sheet metal down to size.

3. Using your width measurement from the first step, use your miter box to cut down your pieces of wood lathe into four pieces that will be used to hold the metal in place.

4. Place your cut metal sheet in the back of the window. Place one piece of lathe at each end and two spaced out through the center. Use your hammer and nails to attach your woods strips to the frame by hammering the nails in at an angle. Continue until all the strips are secure.

5. Attach your picture-hanging hardware according to the directions included with the packaging.

TIPS & RECOMMENDATIONS

If you'd like to leave the glass in your vintage window intact, just add the galvanized metal to the back as a decorative background and use the glass as a wipe board.

BASIC WALL DISPLAY SHELF

A long time ago, I found a vintage box that appeared to be a tray. When I got it home, I actually decided to hang it on the wall and use it as a shelf instead. There was just enough depth inside the tray to feature some of my favorite pieces, but I loved the ability to add things along the top as well as inside. With this Basic Wall Display Shelf, you get all of the same advantages of the vintage tray I found, but with the added character of a galvanized back. And of course, you could also use this as a tray, just like the vintage one I love. ▶

Materials

- 4 pieces of wood for the frame, 2 pieces cut to the larger-side length of your sheet metal and 2 pieces cut to the shorter-side length of your sheet metal (The wood I used was 1" thick and 2½" wide. I also used wood that had a rustic finish already. If you are working with new wood, stain it before you start.)
- Work gloves
- Eye protection

- Drill
- Sandpaper
- Screw gun
- 4 wood screws
- 12" × 24" piece of sheet metal
- 20 sheet metal screws
- 1 French cleat (optional)
- Rubber gloves
- Wood stain
- Stain cloth

1. Place the ends of one of the larger and one of the smaller pieces of wood adjacent to each other, forming a 90-degree angle. Wear your work gloves and eye protection and use your drill to create a pilot hole that goes through the outside piece of wood into the inside piece of wood. Then remove your drill from the wood. Use your sandpaper to lightly sand the edges and corners to make sure they are smooth.

2. Use your screw gun to attach the two pieces together with a wood screw, leaving the screw just a little loose. Repeat for each of the corners. Then, once all of the screws are in, line the corners up with your sheet metal and tighten all four corners to ensure that your sheet metal sits inside the framework of the wood and does not hang out over the edge.

3. Place the sheet metal on the back of the wood and use your screw gun to attach it to the wood with sheet metal screws.

4. If desired, use your screw gun to attach a French cleat to help you hang your shelf.

5. Put on your rubber gloves and apply stain with the stain cloth to the cut edges of your wood to blend them in with the rest of the wood.

TIPS & RECOMMENDATIONS

When creating this project, I purposefully used a size of sheet metal that could be purchased right off the shelf without any cutting. However, with a straightedge and a pair of metal snips, you can cut a piece of sheet metal down to any size of your choice. The easiest size to find is 24" × 36" and you can size down from there. You could also join two pieces and have the seam hidden by an extra shelf. For this project, using a chop saw will be the quickest and easiest way to cut your wood, but if you don't have access to one, a miter box will work perfectly well.

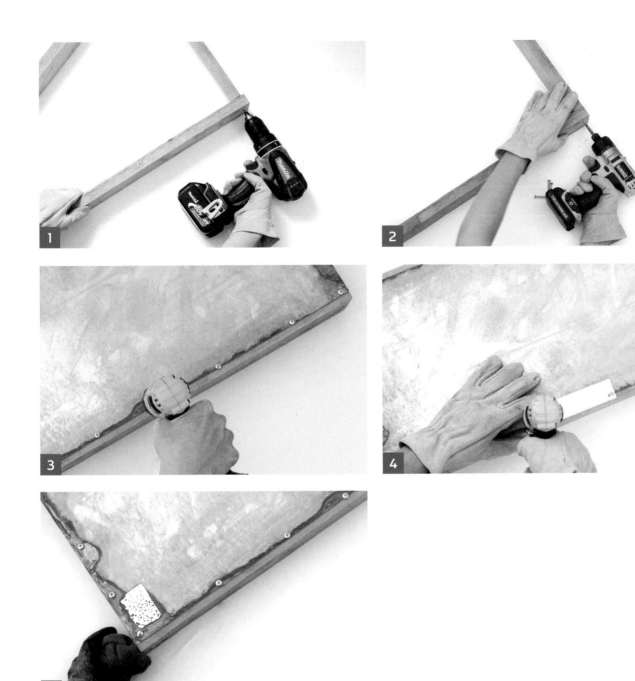

FEED PAN CLOCK

I kept looking for a wall clock that had clean lines and some vintage character, but I kept coming up disappointed and empty-handed. So, I turned to a DIY option to get just what I wanted. I chose to work with a white classic clock face, but that is just one option. The style of the numbers and the hands can set the whole direction of your clock, or you could even leave the numbers off all together or use something like dominoes or Scrabble pieces in their place. ▸

Materials

- Ruler
- Pencil
- Feed pan (the one I used had a 12¾" opening)
- Clock kit
- Drill
- Eye protection
- Work gloves
- Metal file
- Craft glue
- Paintbrush (I used an artist brush sized for detail painting)
- White gloss enamel paint
- Straight pin (optional)

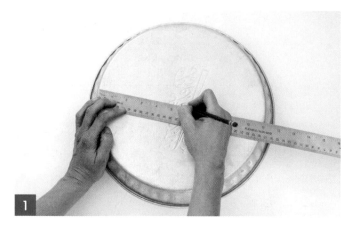

1. Use your ruler and pencil to find and mark the center point of the bottom of your feed pan.

2. Open up your clock kit and measure the width of the stem of this kit. Put on your eye protection and work gloves. Use your drill with a drill bit sized to the width of the stem to create a hole in your center point, then use your metal file to smooth out any rough edges in the cut metal. Insert your clock kit and add a dab of glue to the stem, away from any of the mechanisms, to keep it in place.

3. Separate each of the numbers and the clock hands and use your paintbrush to paint them with the white gloss enamel paint. Do not add too much paint as it will cause the numbers to stick to the surface below them.

4. Add the hands to the clock mechanism and glue the numbers in place. Start with 12 and 6, then add 3 and 9, and finish with the remaining numbers. If desired, you can use a straight pin to apply the glue, which can be helpful when attaching such small pieces.

GALVANIZED MIRROR FRAME

I have seen beautiful galvanized mirrors in stores or catalogs so many times, but the price always seemed too high. I was determined to figure out a way to make it work through a DIY project, and standing in the pet section of a farm-supply store, I finally figured out that a feed tray was the best place to start. By applying an aging technique and following a few very simple steps, I was able to get the exact mirror I wanted for a fraction of the price. The best part is, if you get tired of this mirror on your wall, it can easily be used as a beautiful tray. ▶

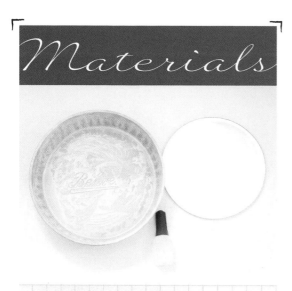

- Heavy-duty craft glue appropriate for mirrors
- Craft mirror or mirrored candle tray that fits inside your feed tray (the one I used had a 10" diameter)
- Galvanized feed tray (the one I used had a 12¾" opening)

1. Add glue to the back side of the mirror.

2. Center the mirror on the inside of the feed tray and hold it in place for about 1 minute. Allow glue to dry per package instructions.

TIPS & RECOMMENDATIONS

Hanging a mirror like this is not as difficult as it might seem. Simply attach several picture-hanging strips to the back of the mirror and hold in place according to the directions on the packaging.

RUSTIC LETTER SIGN

Words can be powerful and inspiring. Whether they are words from a loved one, a quote from someone famous, or just a favorite saying, decorating your space with words that can be seen every day is the perfect way to personalize your home. This project lets you choose whichever words you want—from something as small as spelling out a child's name to as large as the lyrics of a song—and is truly only limited by your imagination. I chose to add letters to a stained piece of plywood, but you could easily paint the wood or cover it in fabric. Or instead of wood, you could choose to use a white or a burlap canvas. ▶

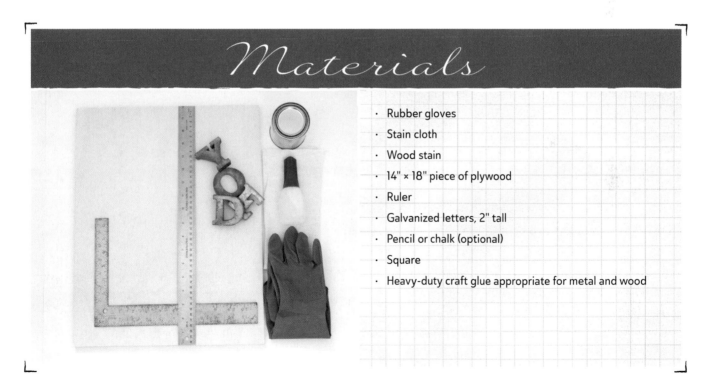

Materials

- Rubber gloves
- Stain cloth
- Wood stain
- 14" × 18" piece of plywood
- Ruler
- Galvanized letters, 2" tall
- Pencil or chalk (optional)
- Square
- Heavy-duty craft glue appropriate for metal and wood

1. Put your rubber gloves on to protect your hands, dip your stain cloth into the stain, and stain your plywood. Be sure to wipe in the direction of the wood grain. Once applied, wipe off any extra stain within a few minutes of applying. Follow the package directions on your stain to allow for proper drying time before moving on to the next step.

2. Use your ruler to line up your letters and determine your layout on the plywood. It is best to line up the left side of your words first. If you desire, you could make a pencil or chalk mark for reference.

3. Line up your bottom word with the square, using the placement of the first letter determined in step 2 as your guide.

4. Glue each letter to the plywood.

5. Move up the plywood, using your square to keep your letters straight, until you have completed all of your words. Let the glue dry according to package instructions and then you are ready to enjoy your sign.

TIPS & RECOMMENDATIONS

This project would work great as a gift. Imagine a wedding present with the new family's last name or a baby gift with a quote from a favorite storybook.

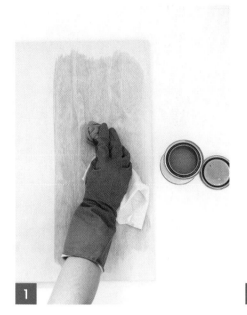

Chapter 3
RUSTIC METAL LIGHTING

One of my favorite things to do before guests come to our home is turn on table lamps and lights and light candles. It is just these little touches that make a room more welcoming and comfortable. Whether you are decorating a room from scratch or just looking to do an update, lighting is one of the final layers to bring a room together. I liken it to choosing the right jewelry for an outfit; the right lighting brings in that final touch. It is an inexpensive way to customize a room and make it unique.

Rustic-style lighting can work in almost any style of decorating. It can be used to further an already rustic room or provide a perfect contrast to a more modern or traditional style. By finding or creating pieces that match your unique tastes, galvanized lighting can bring character and depth to a room. From overhead lighting to luminaries to a lantern, this chapter covers projects to make your home truly special.

MILK CAN TABLE LAMP

I love anytime I can add a little bit of farmhouse style without going overboard, and using a vintage milk can to make a lamp brings just the perfect amount of character and interest to our home. I added mine to a nightstand in our guest room, but it could move to almost any room. Don't be intimidated at the possibility of making a lamp; the lamp kit makes it really simple, and the only tools this project needs are a drill and maybe a pair of pliers. ▶

Materials

- Pliers (optional)
- Milk can
- Eye protection
- Drill with hole saw attachment sized to the neck of the lamp kit
- Work gloves
- Metal file
- Lamp kit
- Lampshade sized in proportion to your milk can (the one I used is 10" high with a top diameter of 12")
- Harp (optional)

1. If necessary, use a pair of pliers to remove the top handle from the cap of the milk can.

2. Put on your eye protection and use your drill with a hole saw attachment to drill a hole in the center of the cap of your milk can equal to the diameter of the neck of the lamp kit.

3. Use a regular drill bit (large enough to accommodate your cord) to drill a hole on the back of the milk can about ½" up from the bottom of the can. Wearing your work gloves, file the opening until smooth.

4. Thread the cord through the back of the milk can and up and out of the hole in the top.

5. Assemble the lamp kit's electrical components according to the directions.

6. Add your lampshade. Depending on your lamp kit and the style of your shade, you may need to add a harp before adding your electrical components. **Note:** A harp is made up of the metal pieces that attach to the shade and hold it in place. To attach, simply slide it on the stem that is holding the electrical components in place. Some shades do not use a harp; they clip onto your light bulb. Only use a harp if your shade does not clip onto the light bulb.

2

3

4

TIPS & RECOMMENDATIONS

Customize your lamp even further by adding trim or stenciling your lampshade. Also, if you can't find a vintage milk can, reproductions can easily be found.

END CAP SOY CANDLES

I first made my own soy candles a few years ago and I have loved making them ever since. Soy candles burn clean and fresh, and you can customize them with your own fragrance. They also make great gifts for holidays because you can easily make only a few or a whole bunch of them at a time. Here, you'll learn how to make your own soy candles, and while you've probably seen them done many times in glass jars, you'll love this fresh and unexpected approach of using a galvanized stove end cap. ▸

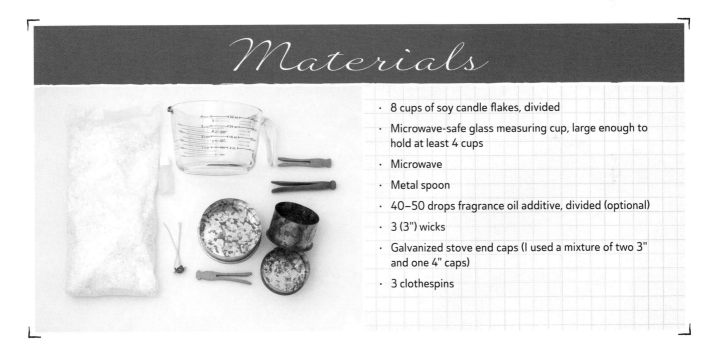

Materials

- 8 cups of soy candle flakes, divided
- Microwave-safe glass measuring cup, large enough to hold at least 4 cups
- Microwave
- Metal spoon
- 40–50 drops fragrance oil additive, divided (optional)
- 3 (3") wicks
- Galvanized stove end caps (I used a mixture of two 3" and one 4" caps)
- 3 clothespins

1

5

6

1. Fill 4 cups of candle flakes into a measuring cup. Work with 4 cups of wax flakes at a time when melting. Working with smaller batches allows for easier monitoring when it melts. If you end up with any extra melted wax when you are done making your candles, you can store it in a glass container to melt at a future date or wait for it to cool and dispose of it.

2. Microwave the flakes on high for 1 minute and then stir the mixture with a metal spoon.

3. Microwave the flakes for an additional 4 minutes or until completely liquefied. **Note:** You have about 15 minutes to work with the wax before it begins to set.

4. If desired, add 20–25 drops of fragrance oil additive for every 4 cups of wax.

5. Place the wick in the stove end cap so that the metal clip on one end sits at the bottom and in the center. Place the clothespin over the edges of the end cap and slide your wick into the opening. This will hold the wick in place while the wax sets.

6. Put your stove end caps on a cleanable or disposable surface and pour your liquid wax into your stove end caps until it's about 1/4" to 1/2" from the top. Let the candles sit overnight to completely set.

7. Repeat each step with the remaining 4 cups of soy candle flakes and discard any remaining wax once all your end caps have been filled.

DRY-BRUSHED CANDLE TRAY

When I had my first apartment and absolutely no money, the only way I knew how to brighten up a room was to splurge on some inexpensive candles. I wish I had this idea back then! By using an unexpected item, like a mud pan, and a little bit of paint, in just a few minutes you can have a pretty candle tray that is sure to add a special touch in any room. ▶

Materials

- 1 (1") foam paintbrush
- White paint (I used chalky style paint)
- Paper towels
- 12" mud pan (found at hardware stores or online)
- Quick-drying glue
- 2 drawer handles
- Pillar candles (I used 4 candles of varying sizes)
- About 2 cups of Epsom salts (optional)

1. Dip your foam paintbrush in just a little bit of paint.

2. Brush off as much paint as you can on a paper towel.

3. Lightly paint the outside surfaces of the mud pan and let it dry according to package instructions before moving to the next step.

4. Use your quick-drying glue to attach the handles on the sides of the mud pan; hold them in place for a few minutes. The handles should be centered on the sides and placed about 1" down from the top. Follow all glue package directions for dry times.

5. Insert your pillar candles into the mud pan. If your pillar candles are not fitting as well as you would like, or you would like them to sit up higher, add some Epsom salts to the base to lift them up.

TIPS & RECOMMENDATIONS

I chose to paint the pan with white paint, but you can use any color to accent your room.

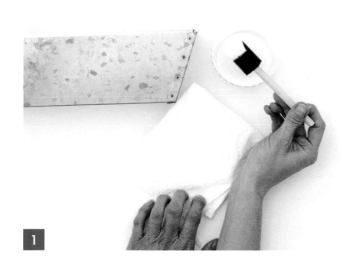

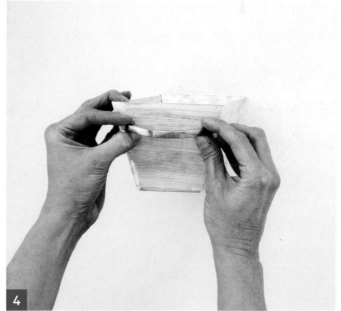

PENDANT LIGHT

I have a very sentimental attachment to maple buckets since my husband grew up on a farm making maple syrup and we now make our own as a family business. Because of this, I have always wanted to find a way to incorporate a maple bucket into our home décor, and when we redid a space in our home, I knew it was the perfect place to add this maple bucket Pendant Light. This project is surprisingly easy and quick to complete. It uses a pendant light kit to eliminate the step of electrical work, but if you want to hardwire your fixture, as we chose to do, that's a great option. ▸

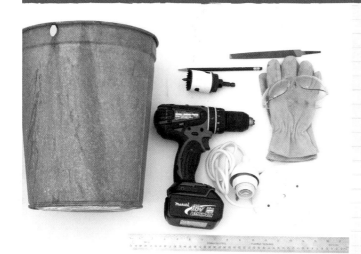

Materials

- Ruler
- Sap bucket
- Pencil
- Work gloves
- Eye protection
- Drill with hole saw attachment sized to your pendant light kit stem
- Metal file
- Pendant light kit

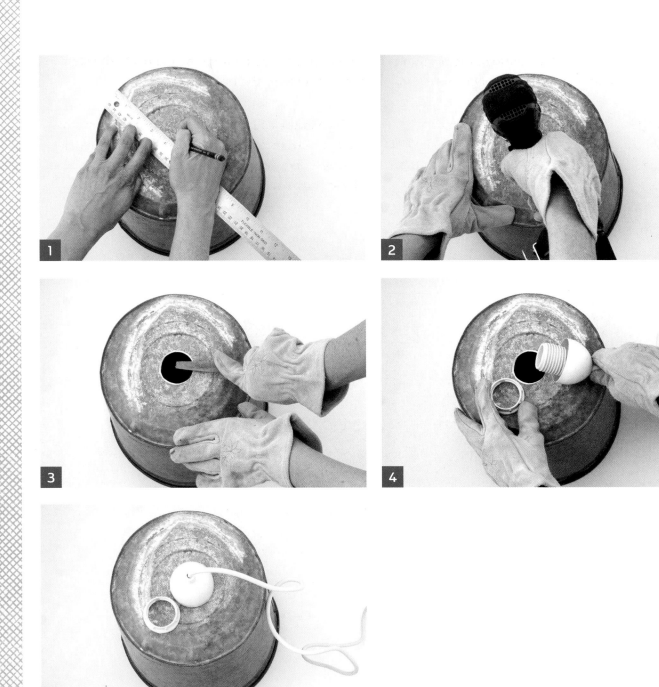

1. Use your ruler to find the center of the bottom of your bucket and mark it with your pencil.

2. Put on your work gloves and eye protection, place the hole saw attachment on your drill, line it up with your center mark, and drill a hole in the bottom of the bucket.

3. Keep your work gloves on and use your metal file to smooth any rough edges.

4. Remove the collar from the pendant light stem and insert it into the opening.

5. Thread the collar back on to the stem from inside the bucket to hold the fixture in place, then install your light fixture according to the directions on the pendant kit packaging.

TIPS & RECOMMENDATIONS

I used a vintage sap bucket for this project, but the same project would work with a vintage or a new galvanized bucket of almost any size and shape.

CANDLE LUMINARIES

Whether indoors or outdoors, there is something so magical about a space lit up with candle luminaries. The pattern possibilities are endless, and I love when the light casts the pattern out into the space. Whether you do one, three, five, or enough to line your whole walkway, luminaries create a beautiful welcome to your home. I love the idea of doing these with galvanized buckets in a mixture of sizes and shapes to create a rustic, elegant display. ▶

Materials

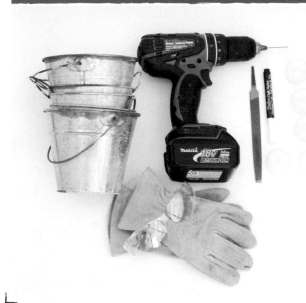

- Galvanized buckets in your choice of sizes and shapes (I used a total of 5)
- Chalk marker
- Work gloves
- Eye protection
- Drill (the bit depends on what size opening you prefer)
- Metal file
- 1 votive candle per bucket

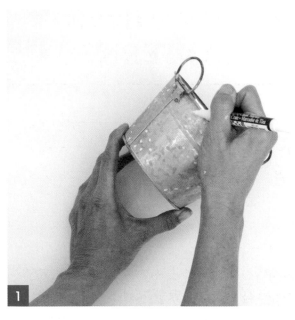

1. Draw your desired pattern for holes onto your galvanized buckets with your chalk marker.

2. Put the buckets on a disposable surface that will catch the drilling dust and use your drill to drill a hole in each of your markings.

3. Put on your work gloves and eye protection and use a metal file to smooth down all of your sharp edges. Once all the holes are filed, place a votive candle in each bucket. Place your luminaries outdoors to light up a space or gather them on a table to enjoy indoors.

TIPS & RECOMMENDATIONS

Drilling all of these holes can be time-consuming, so find a comfortable spot and just take your time. Please be extra sure to use work gloves when filing and take extra care to smooth all of the sharp edges as they really can be dangerous.

GALVANIZED LANTERNS

Sometimes DIY projects are complicated with lots of steps and directions. Sometimes they are simple, and the beauty is in looking at an item in a new way. When I saw the feed scoop used in this project, it immediately looked like a wall lantern to me. With the simple addition of a few pieces and proper installation, it can become a perfect focal point to your living room, or you can install this lantern outdoors to bring light and character to an outdoor seating area. ▶

Materials

- Drill
- Feed scoop
- 1 wood screw
- Mason jar or other heat-safe candle vessel (I used a quart-size wide-mouth jar)
- Votive candle

1. Use your drill to drill a small pilot hole in the back panel of your scoop, then use a wood screw to attach your scoop (open-side up) to your wall, preferably in a wall stud.

2. Add your Mason jar or other heat-safe candle vessel to the scoop. Add your candle and light it.

TIPS & RECOMMENDATIONS

This project does not need to be hung. It would work just as beautifully on a mantel or side table. Also, the Mason jar does not need to be clear. You can now find new Mason jars in blue, green, and even purple.

Chapter 4
RUSTIC METAL STORAGE OPTIONS

If there is one thing that is likely universal in all homes, it is the need to find useful storage and space. I always try to figure out new places and ways to store things, which can be an art form. I figure there is no reason why filling these nooks and crannies for storage should just be functional. Why not make it pretty and unique as well? Here you'll find projects that repurpose galvanized metal materials into small and large storage containers and vintage treasures to help organize your home. From the smallest items that need corralling in the bathroom to storage that can also serve as a coffee table, this chapter will guide you through creative ways to control the clutter.

COFFEE TABLE ON CASTERS

Sometimes choosing a coffee table that fits a smaller space can be challenging, so why not make your own that fits perfectly and provides storage as well? This simple tutorial will take you about 15 minutes and allow you to customize your space perfectly. I used a 24" galvanized bin, but you can use whatever size best fits your space. To personalize your piece further, you could add a stencil to the top or add handles to make accessing storage even easier. ▶

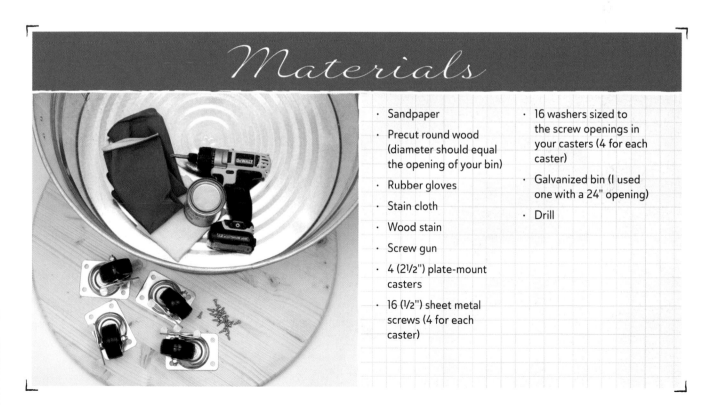

Materials

- Sandpaper
- Precut round wood (diameter should equal the opening of your bin)
- Rubber gloves
- Stain cloth
- Wood stain
- Screw gun
- 4 (2½") plate-mount casters
- 16 (½") sheet metal screws (4 for each caster)
- 16 washers sized to the screw openings in your casters (4 for each caster)
- Galvanized bin (I used one with a 24" opening)
- Drill

1. Lightly sand your wood top to remove any rough spots and wipe off any dust with a cloth. Put on your rubber gloves and use your stain cloth to stain one side of your wood top, being sure to apply the stain in the direction of the wood grain. Wipe off any excess stain and allow it dry according to the package directions. Once the stain is dry, repeat on the other side of the wood top until it is completely stained and dry, according to the package directions.

2. Use your screw gun to attach each of the casters with sheet metal screws and washers by placing each caster on the bottom of the bin and lining up a washer with each screw opening on the caster. Place your screw in the opening and use your drill to drive the screw in, which will hold the washer and caster in place. A pilot hole is not needed because the sheet metal screws will "grab" the metal as they are driven in. Repeat with each caster, placing them at four equally spaced spots.

TIPS & RECOMMENDATIONS

When picking out your casters, you will find that rotating-and-locking casters are much more expensive. For this project, it is worth considering purchasing them anyway. It is great to be able to easily move the table and then lock it in place.

BUCKET WALL SHELF

I have always wanted to hang a galvanized bucket on the wall, but I also wanted it to be functional. After experimenting with how to hold it on the wall and how to best use it, I finally came up with a project that worked: this Bucket Wall Shelf! I love the storage functionality and I love the mix of the galvanized metal with rustic wood. And the bonus with this project is that it can also be used as a magnet board. ▶

Materials

- Tape measure
- Galvanized bucket (the one I used was about 18" in diameter at the opening)
- Wood shelf about ½" thick and 8" deep or what fits best inside your bucket (length will be cut to fit according to width of your bucket)
- Pencil

- Square
- Work gloves
- Eye protection
- Chop saw or jigsaw
- Rubber gloves
- Stain cloth

- Wood stain
- Drill
- Screw gun
- 7 wood screws
- Level

1. Use your tape measure to measure the inside diameter of the base of the galvanized bucket. This will be the shorter length of your shelf.

2. Measure the depth of your shelf (mine was 8"). Measure up from the bottom of the bucket on the inside to the depth of your shelf and mark this measurement on each side of the bucket with a pencil.

3. Measure across the bucket at the two marks you just made. This is the longest length of your shelf.

4. Use a pencil and mark the longest length on one of your shelf's edges.

5. Use your measuring tape and find and mark the center point of this longest length.

6. Use your square and a pencil and draw a line from this center point across to the other side of the board across from the first mark, which will be the shelf's shorter-length side. ▶

TIPS & RECOMMENDATIONS

This project is perfect for your guest bathroom as well. Roll and tuck hand towels and wash cloths to be readily available for your guests. You can even add toiletries on the shelf to make the perfect guest welcome.

7. Using your width measurement from step 1, divide the width in half and measure out half that length in each direction from your center point from step 6 and mark it with your pencil.

8. Use the edge of your square and a pencil and draw a line to connect the ends of the longer length with the ends of the shorter length. This will give you your angle for cutting the sides of your shelf.

9. Put on your work gloves and eye protection, line up your angle carefully, and cut with a chop saw. If you do not have access to a chop saw, you could also use a jigsaw. Place your board inside your bucket to ensure your cuts are correct and it fits.

10. Put on your rubber gloves, dip the stain cloth in the wood stain, and apply the stain in the direction of the wood grain. Be sure to wipe off any excess stain. Let the stain dry according to package directions.

11. Place the stained shelf inside the bucket and measure to double-check that it is centered from top to bottom.

12. Use your drill to drill a pilot hole and then use your screw gun to attach one screw on each side from the outside of the bucket into the wood shelf. Place your screw about 1" in from the bottom side of the bucket, making sure it's lined up with the placement of the shelf. After the first screw is attached on each side, use your level to ensure the board is straight. Then add an additional screw in each side about 1" down from the top end of your wood shelf. Finally, measure with your tape measure where the shelf sits relative to the bottom of the bucket and then transfer that measurement to the back of the bucket. Then use your screw gun to attach three screws from the back side into the shelf, one in the middle and one on either side about 3"–4" from the middle.

ART CADDY

We are a marker, colored pencil, and crayon family. Even as a grown woman, my dad still fills my Christmas stocking with colorful markers. I often spend time with my daughters just coloring. We are always grabbing a bunch of bins filled with markers, colored pencils, and crayons and passing them back and forth. I was determined to figure out a way to create an art caddy that we could set right in the middle of us so that we all could easily grab what we want. Of course, it is even better that I figured out how to do it with galvanized buckets. And this Art Caddy is perfect for organizing any desk, even if you don't have kids. Fill it with pencils, pens, highlighters, and even scissors! ▸

Materials

- 5 galvanized buckets in various sizes
  (I used buckets in the following sizes: top: 4" diameter × 4" tall, top spacer: 2" diameter × 2" tall, center: 6" diameter × 4" tall, bottom spacer: 4" diameter × 4" tall, bottom: 8" diameter × 4½" tall)

- Heavy-duty craft glue appropriate for use on metal

1. The most challenging part of this project is figuring out the perfect mix of buckets. It is really a game of stacking and seeing what lines up best. Start with your largest bucket (8" × 4½") and glue your second-smallest bucket (4" × 4") upside down and centered inside.

2. Then glue your second-largest bucket (6" × 4") to the top of the upside-down bucket, making a second tier. Glue your smallest bucket (2" × 2") upside down, inside, and centered in the second-largest bucket (on your second tier).

3. Glue your final bucket (4" × 4") centered on top of the upside-down bucket on the second tier. Follow the glue instructions for drying times.

VINTAGE MILK CRATE STOOL

I have had a long love affair with anything vintage, especially when it is made of galvanized metal, which means that I could not pass up this galvanized milk crate when I found it. Even though I had no immediate plans for it, I stored it and just kept looking at it from time to time. Then, one day, inspiration struck. It would work perfectly as an extra stool to tuck under our console table. With a little bit of some reproduction vintage details, I was able to create a one-of-a-kind stool for our kitchen, and so can you! ▸

Materials

 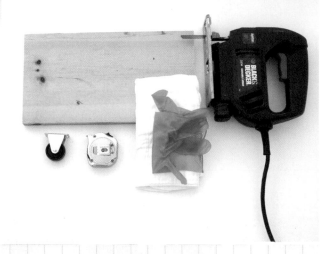

- Galvanized milk crate (the one I used is 14" × 10" × 11")
- Tape measure
- Jigsaw
- Plywood cut to the size of the top opening of the milk crate (the piece I used is 14" × 10")
- Sandpaper
- Rubber gloves
- Stain cloth
- Wood stain
- Image or words printed onto an 8½" × 11" sheet of printer paper

- Pencil
- Painter's tape
- Permanent marker
- Drill
- 4 (1½") wood screws
- 16 (1") wood screws
- 4 (½") plate-mount casters
- 2 small strips of wood measured and cut to fit the bottom of your crate (optional, for attaching casters; I used pieces of lathe that were 1½" wide × 11" long)

1. Measure the length and depth of the top of your crate and use a jigsaw to cut your plywood to these dimensions. Use your sandpaper to lightly sand the edges. An optional idea is to round the corners when you are cutting.

2. Put on your rubber gloves and use your stain cloth to stain one side of your wood, being sure to apply the stain in the direction of the wood grain. Wipe off any excess stain and allow to dry according to package instructions. Once the stain is dry, repeat on the other side of the wood, until both sides are completely stained and dry according to package instructions.

3. Take the paper on which you printed your desired words or image. Turn the paper over and use your pencil to shade all of the area where the print shows. I went back and forth and then from top to bottom to make sure it was fully covered.

4. Place your paper, with the printed side face-up, on your wood and tape it in place with your painter's tape. Then trace the outline of all of the letters or images with your pencil. This will transfer the lead from the back of your paper onto the wood. ▶

TIPS & RECOMMENDATIONS

If you are unable to find a vintage galvanized milk crate, you might be able to find a wood one with galvanized edges. Or, you can use the tutorial in this chapter for the Faux Vintage Crate and add a top and casters.

5. Use your permanent marker to fill in your traced outline.

6. Use your drill to attach your plywood to your crate by inserting 1 (1½") screw at each corner.

7. Attach your casters to each corner of the base of the crate by using a drill to drill a pilot hole at each corner of the caster. Then use a screwdriver bit to drill the 1" screws through the pilot holes. If there is no wood or metal to drill into, lay the small wood strips on opposite sides of the bottom of the crate, use your drill to drill pilot holes through the sides of the crate and into the wood strips at each end of the wood strip, then attach the strips with screws through the pilot holes. Then attach your casters to the wood with screws.

FAUX VINTAGE CRATE

I have been picking up vintage crates at yard sales for years. Over the last few years, however, I have found that they have become harder to come by, and when I find them, they are pretty expensive. I decided to set out to make this new crate that had the charm and character of a vintage one. Adding the text to the sides and the galvanized brackets to the corners gives this project the vintage touch a new crate needs. ▶

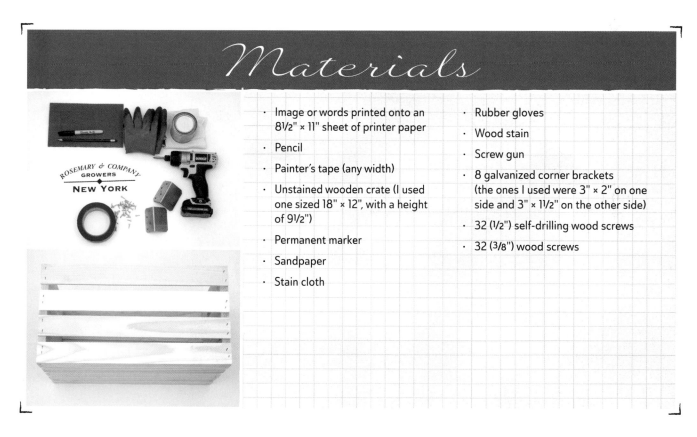

Materials

- Image or words printed onto an 8½" × 11" sheet of printer paper
- Pencil
- Painter's tape (any width)
- Unstained wooden crate (I used one sized 18" × 12", with a height of 9½")
- Permanent marker
- Sandpaper
- Stain cloth
- Rubber gloves
- Wood stain
- Screw gun
- 8 galvanized corner brackets (the ones I used were 3" × 2" on one side and 3" × 1½" on the other side)
- 32 (½") self-drilling wood screws
- 32 (⅜") wood screws

1. Take the paper on which you printed your desired words or image. Turn the paper over and use your pencil to shade all of the area where the print shows. I went back and forth and then from top to bottom to make sure it was fully covered.

2. Use your painter's tape to tape your paper in place on your crate, with the printed side face up. Then trace the outline of your design with your pencil. This will transfer the lead from the back of the paper to your wood in your desired pattern.

3. Fill in the design with your permanent marker.

4. To create a vintage look, sand the area with sandpaper.

5. Wipe the area with your dry stain cloth. Do not be worried if the marker spreads; it will blend in with the stain.

6. Put on your rubber gloves, dip your cloth in your stain, and cover your entire crate with stain, applying it in the direction of the wood grain. Remove any excess stain and allow the stain to dry according to package instructions.

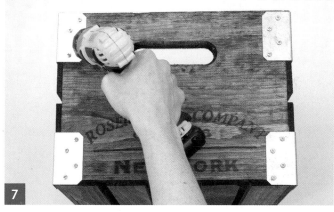

7. Use your screw gun to attach the brackets to the outside of each of the corners. Use the ½" screws on the ends of the crate and the ⅜" screws on the sides of the crate, as the wood on the sides will likely be thinner.

TIPS & RECOMMENDATIONS

Test your marker on the bottom of your crate first to see how much the ink bleeds. Always start filling in your design from the inside so as to not bleed too far out of the lines.

LIDDED STORAGE CONTAINERS

When storing items in your bathroom or craft room, it is ideal to have the things you use every day easily accessible and out of drawers and cabinets. However, that can easily lead to clutter and mess. Fortunately, you can use small galvanized buckets to keep all kinds of things in their place, and, by adding a cover, you can keep things neat and organized. ▶

Materials

- Rubber gloves
- Stain cloth
- Wood stain
- 3 wood plaques or wood crafting circles sized to fit the opening of each of the buckets
- Ruler
- Drill
- 3 cabinet knobs (1 for each bucket) with screws for attaching
- 3 small galvanized buckets (I used ones with 3½" and 5" openings)

1. Put on your rubber gloves and use your stain cloth to stain one side of your wood plaques, being sure to apply the stain in the direction of the wood grain. Wipe off any excess stain and allow it to dry according to package instructions. Once the stain is dry, repeat on the other side of the plaques, until all are completely stained and dry, according to package instructions.

2. Use your ruler to measure and find the center point of each plaque, then use your drill to create a hole at that center point in each plaque.

3. Attach a knob to each plaque, place the plaques on top of your buckets, and begin organizing.

TIPS & RECOMMENDATIONS

These canisters are perfect for storing cotton swabs, cotton balls, and dental floss in the bathroom. They work equally great in your craft room for buttons, thread, and scrapbooking materials.

TOY STORAGE ON CASTERS

One of the biggest challenges with a house full of kids is keeping control of the toys. To avoid stepping on building blocks or tripping on baby dolls, having a place to keep toys off the floor, yet still accessible, is a necessity. This project shows the easy steps to create a toy storage bin that not only looks great but is easy for kids to use. With no cover on top and wheels for easy movement, kids can pick up after themselves with ease. And with a simple painting technique, you can customize this project to suit your room. ▸

Materials

- Painter's tape (I used 1" tape)
- Galvanized bucket (I used one with a 14" opening)
- 1" foam paintbrush
- Craft paint in the color of your choice
- 4 (1½") plate-mount casters
- Heavy-duty craft glue appropriate for metal

1. Wrap painter's tape along the top edge of your galvanized bucket. Then, about 2" down the bucket, wrap another piece of tape. Because of the shape of the bucket, your tape will not lay smooth; just make sure the tape is smooth, straight, and secure on the side you are painting.

2. Use your foam paintbrush to brush a thin coat of paint between your taped lines.

3. Let the paint dry according to package instructions. Apply two additional coats to ensure full coverage.

4. Next, paint the inside bottom of your bin with a thin coat of paint. Let the paint dry according to package instructions, then apply two more coats, letting each coat dry between applications, to ensure full coverage.

5. Under normal circumstances you would use screws to attach your casters. However, that would leave the screws protruding through the inside, which is a hazard. Instead, attach each of your casters with heavy-duty craft glue and follow the directions for drying times.

TIPS & RECOMMENDATIONS

When your kids grow out of the need for this type of storage, don't throw it away. Use this bucket for shoes by your door, bulk items in your pantry, or even items in your closet.

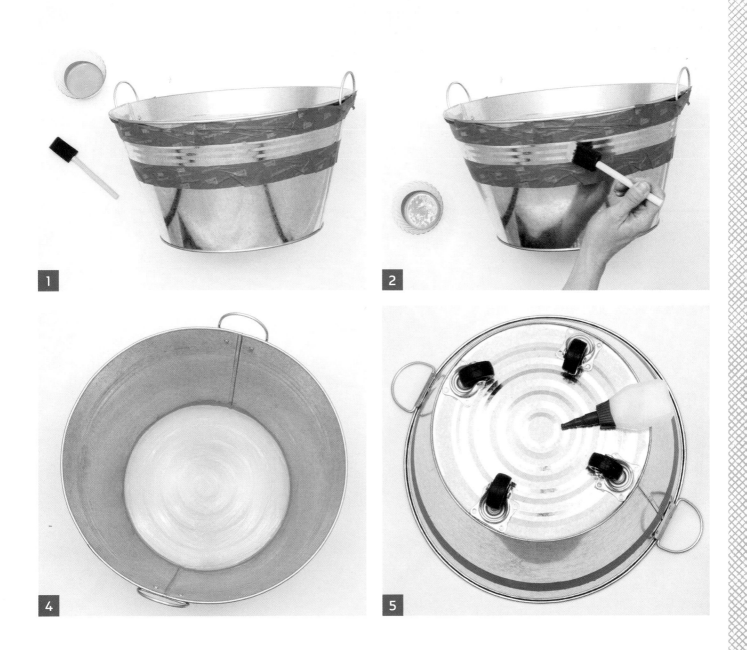

Chapter 5

RUSTIC METAL PLANTERS

One of my favorite—and one of the easiest—ways to use galvanized containers is as planters. Each spring, we fill our front and back porches with annuals tucked in vintage and new galvanized buckets. I love the contrast of the color and the texture of the flowers with the rustic texture of the galvanized metal. In fact, one of the first major DIY projects we ever took on was the Three-Tiered Outdoor Planter that you'll find in this chapter.

Over time, we have started bringing some plants in vintage containers indoors as well, and I love them indoors just as much. In our kitchen, we now have herbs at our fingertips in a beautiful farm-styled planter, and succulents are featured in our family room. In this chapter you'll learn the different ways you can create creative, rustic metal planters that you can showcase both inside your home and out.

HOUSE NUMBER PLANTER

Sometimes a project doesn't have to be complicated to be stunning. My favorite projects are the ones where you can get a custom look in just minutes. This project that teaches you how to create a House Number Planter definitely falls into that category. Displaying your house number is important, so you may as well make it look beautiful while you are at it. ▸

Materials

- Plastic house numbers (I used 3" numbers)
- Galvanized bucket (I used one 13" high with a 13" opening)
- Screw gun

- Sheet metal screws (you will need two for each number)
- Drill
- Gravel, potting soil, and plants or garden-center pot

1. Line up your numbers on your bucket where you want them placed. I used the lines on the bucket as my guide to make sure the numbers were straight and even.

2. Use your screw gun to attach each of your numbers with the sheet metal screws. Be sure to hold each number tightly in place while attaching or the number will spin out.

3. Use your drill to drill several drainage holes in the bottom of the galvanized bucket. Add gravel to the base for drainage and to weigh down your planter. Next, add potting soil and your plants. Another option would be to place an existing garden-center pot directly into the bucket.

END CAP SUCCULENT GARDEN

I love adding plants throughout my home. Succulents have become the latest "it girl" in the plant world, and when planted in galvanized containers, they're guaranteed to give your home décor a boost. Not only are succulents a lot harder to kill than other plants, but they come in all types of interesting shapes and colors. In trying to find an interesting planter, I stumbled upon stove end caps in a hardware store and found that they make the perfect vessel for succulents. Not only do they look great, but they are inexpensive and come in many different sizes to fuel your creativity and complement your personal style. ▶

Materials

- 5 or 6 packs of succulents found at a garden center or hardware store (try to find 3–5 varying types)
- 2 (5") round end caps
- 1 (3") round end cap
- Potting soil

1. Find a surface that will be easy to clean up and remove your succulents from their plastic pots. Place individual plants in the different galvanized end caps. Mix up the variety of plants in each container for interest.

2. Fill in any extra room in the end caps with potting soil and then compact the plants together.

3. Add enough water to keep your plants damp. There aren't any holes for drainage, so be sure not to overwater.

4. Continue to follow the care instructions that came with your plant.

WINDOWSILL HERB PLANTER

I love to use fresh herbs in cooking—the taste is so much better than from a jar. But finding an out-of-the-way place for them in the kitchen can be challenging. Fortunately, this creative Windowsill Herb Planter tucks right on a windowsill without taking up much space. Plus, you have to enjoy using a chicken feeder tray to plant herbs. It is a farmhouse-style piece with a bit of a sense of humor. ▸

Materials

- Chicken feeder tray (the one I used was about 19" long)
- An assortment of herb plants (I used 6 plants)
- Chalk
- Plant markers (I used 1 per plant)

1. Remove the top section of the feeder and plan the layout of your plants.

2. Pull your plants out of their containers and separate them from the extra dirt. Add a layer of extra dirt to the bottom of the feeder.

3. Thread each plant through an opening in the top of the feeder.

4. Reattach the top of the feeder to the base and press each plant into place.

5. Use chalk to label your plant markers with the names of the plants and insert them in the feeder.

TIPS & RECOMMENDATIONS

Because of the angle of the planter, watering your herbs might be tricky. Simply set your feeder in your sink when it is dry and add a little bit of water with the spray nozzle of your faucet. Let the planter sit for a little while, wipe the bottom, then put it back in place.

THREE-TIERED OUTDOOR PLANTER

I made the first version of this project with my husband a few years ago. Since then, we've learned a lot about simplifying the process, so you get to benefit from our mistakes. Having a planter this size is perfect if you want to add flowers at a front entrance or plant herbs or vegetables right outside of your kitchen. ▶

Materials

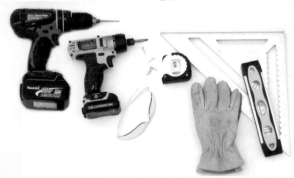

- Work gloves
- Eye protection
- Drill
- 1 large base bucket (the one I used is 24" in diameter at the opening)
- 2 smaller buckets (the ones I used are 7" in diameter at the opening)
- Measuring tape
- Miter box or chop saw
- 1 piece of thin wood (I used lathe that was 1" thick × 2" wide. The two main strips are cut to 24" in length. The angled piece is cut to 10" in length.)

- Door, wood shutter, or piece of plywood (the one I used is 17" wide × 50" tall)
- Screw gun
- 7 sheet metal screws
- Level
- 9 wood screws
- Plate hangers (optional)
- Decorative plates (optional)

1. Put on your work gloves and eye protection and use your drill to create drainage holes in the bottom of each of the galvanized buckets. I drilled seven holes for the smaller buckets and eighteen holes for the largest bucket.

2. Use your measuring tape and measure the diameter of the largest bucket a few inches down from the top. Also measure the diameter of the bottom of the bucket for later use. With your miter box or chop saw, cut two pieces of wood strapping to the length of the bucket's diameter a few inches down from the top (your first measurement). Place the door, shutter, or piece of plywood in the base of the large bucket and sandwich the door between the two pieces of wood strapping board. Use your screw gun to attach each end of the wood strapping to the bucket with a sheet metal screw from the outside of the bucket.

3. Use your level to check that your door is straight.

4. Use your drill to create a pilot hole at the center and at each end of the front side of the strapping, then attach the strapping boards to the door with your screw gun and a wood screw through the pilot holes. ▶

TIPS & RECOMMENDATIONS

Although this project works great for flowers, it is also a great for herbs or even some vegetables. Keep the planter close to your kitchen access and you can easily pick some herbs or vegetables while you are cooking.

5. Lay the door down so you can have access to the bottom of the bucket. Use your screw gun and attach a sheet metal screw through the center of the bottom of the bucket and into the bottom of the door.

6. With your miter box or chop saw, cut a piece of wood strapping as long as the diameter of the bottom of the bucket (your second measurement in step 2). Cut the ends at a 45-degree angle and place the strapping vertically in the bottom of the bucket, on the back side of your door, shutter, or plywood. Use your screw gun to attach the vertical piece of strapping with a wood screw where it meets the horizontal strapping board.

7. Attach each of your two smaller buckets to the front of the door with a screw gun and 1 sheet metal screw.

8. Add a wood screw under each bucket but do not drill it all the way in. The purpose of this screw is to support the weight of the planter.

9. If desired, use plate hangers to attach decorative plates on the back of the door.

TIPS & RECOMMENDATIONS

If you are unable to find a vintage door or shutter, look at new ones. When all else fails, you can also use a piece of plywood with molding attached.

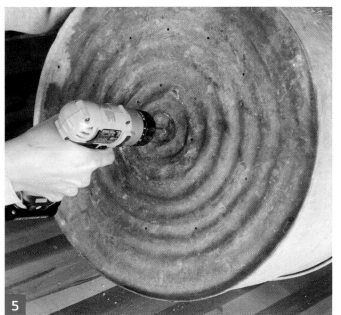

INDOOR HANGING PLANTER

I am a big fan of old-school hanging planters, but every time I look at the instructions for how to do macramé, my eyes begin to glaze over. So, I set out to figure out how to get a similar look but with a simpler process. Of course, I loved it even more when I paired it with a galvanized bucket. I cannot help but love the contrast of the texture of the green twine with the finish of the galvanized bucket. ▸

- 45' of twine, cut into 6 strands of 7½' each
- 1 galvanized bucket with a handle (the one I used is 8" wide at the opening)
- Ruler

1. Gather the six strands of twine together and pull them through the side opening of your bucket where the handle is until you reach the halfway point.

2. Tie a knot over the top of the opening.

3. Gather the two sections of twine together, then divide the now twelve strands into three sets of four strands and braid them loosely.

4. Once you have 18" in length of the braided section, tie a knot. Then repeat on the other side.

5. Join the two sections together where the braiding ends and tie a double knot.

6. Place a potted plant in the bucket and hang it in the location of your choice.

TIPS & RECOMMENDATIONS

You can customize your planter even further by painting its exterior in a pattern with craft paint or paint markers.

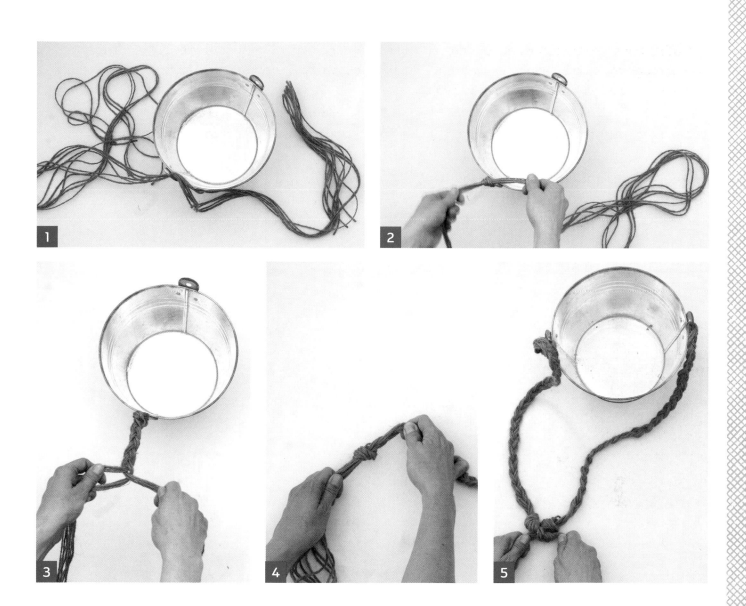

Chapter 6

RUSTIC METAL ACCENTS FOR ENTERTAINING

When we open our home to friends and family, whether for holidays or just an everyday get-together, our guests know not to expect four different kinds of forks and crystal chandeliers. We like to keep things simple, easy, and comfortable. Sometimes we sit at our dining-room table together, but often we set up a buffet and encourage our guests to find a seat that is comfortable. But even though we keep things casual, I still want our home and entertaining setup to be attractive and special. Whether we're entertaining indoors or out, adding galvanized accents brings just the right touch. From keeping your drinks cool to holding your napkin in place to setting up a unique bar, this chapter contains a range of projects, including one that will take minutes, one that requires a power tool or two, and everything in between!

GALVANIZED NAPKIN RINGS

I knew I wanted a simple galvanized touch on my dining table, and a napkin holder seemed the perfect way to do it. But, since I am not a welder, I kept coming up short on what to do. Fortunately, I have a tendency to slowly wander through independent hardware stores and farm-supply stores, focusing on anything with an interesting texture and shape, which is how I came across strap iron. In my weird way of looking at things, it became my "Aha!" moment and the perfect way to simply make a galvanized napkin ring. ▸

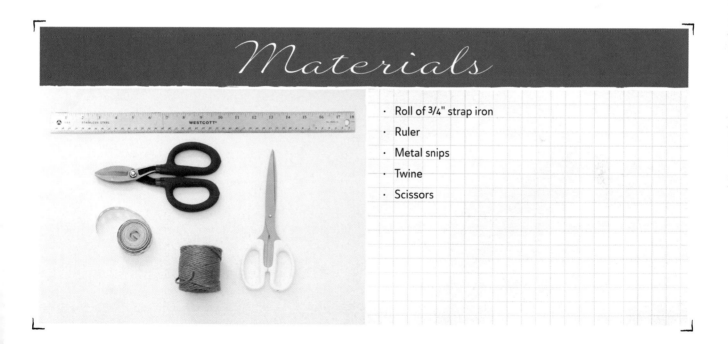

Materials

· Roll of ³⁄₄" strap iron
· Ruler
· Metal snips
· Twine
· Scissors

1. Measure out and cut an 8" strip of strap iron using your metal snips.

2. Fold over one end and then form a circle. Line up the holes at the ends with the folded-over end laying on top.

3. Cut a 5" piece of twine with your scissors.

4. Thread twine from the inside of the ring and tie it in a knot on the outside. Be sure to pull the twine tight to hold the strap iron in place.

5. Trim excess twine with scissors, then thread your napkin through the ring.

6. Repeat until you have your desired number of napkin rings, then set your table.

TIPS & RECOMMENDATIONS

Add another layer of interest to your place settings by using a vintage sap bucket cover as your plate charger.

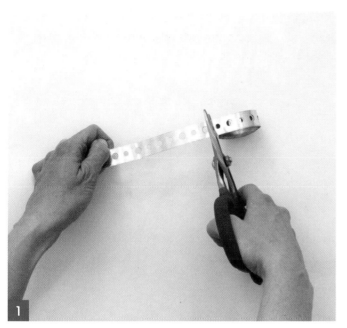

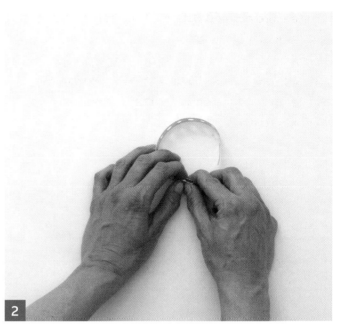

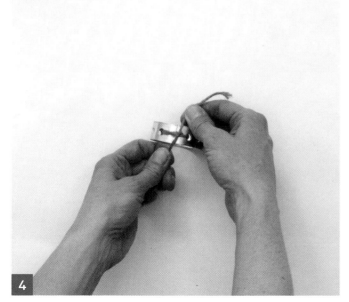

DIP CONTAINER AND TRAY

While most people make their way to the dessert table with speed and grace, I often don't even visit the sweets. I am a chip-and-dip girl through and through and usually save my overeating for the appetizer part of the meal. In fact, sometimes I just make a meal of appetizers. If this sounds familiar, you're going to love this Dip Container and Tray that makes serving chips and dip easy and pretty as well. ▶

Materials

· Rubber gloves

· Stain cloth

· Wood stain

· Unfinished wood tray

· Roll of 3/4" strap iron

· Screw gun

· About 60 (3/4") self-drilling wood screws

· Metal snips

· Small bowl

· Galvanized bucket (slightly larger than the bowl)

1. Put on your rubber gloves and use your stain cloth to stain one side of your wood tray, being sure to apply the stain in the direction of the wood grain. Wipe off any excess stain and allow it to dry according to the package instructions. Once the stain is dry, repeat on the other side of the wood tray until it is completely stained and dry, according to package instructions.

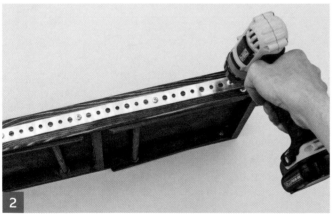

2. Once your tray is dry, roll your strap iron out across one of the outside sides of the tray, starting at a corner. Use your screw gun to insert a wood screw in every other hole of the strap iron.

3. Wrap your strap iron around the sides and each of the tray's corners, being sure to pull the strap iron tight and flush to the tray. Continue to use your screw gun to insert a wood screw in every other hole of the strap iron. When you reach the end, use your metal snips to cut the end free. Then fold over the end and attach your final screw.

4. Pair your tray with an appropriately sized small bowl and slightly larger galvanized bucket. Add ice to the bucket and set your dip bowl into the ice. Set the bucket on your tray and serve your cold dip and yummy chips.

LAZY SUSAN

Every time I find a lazy Susan with just the right details and character I am looking for, the price is way too high for me to justify buying it. So I decided to figure out a way to DIY one with the perfect accents and the character I was looking for. This project is really simple and quick. Assembling all of the needed materials is just about the hardest part. ▶

Materials

- Rubber gloves
- Stain cloth
- Wood stain
- Precut 18" round wood piece
- Ruler
- Screw gun
- About 58 (3/4") self-drilling wood screws
- 3" lazy Susan bearings hardware
- Roll of 3/4" strap iron
- 2 (4 1/2") galvanized cabinet handles

1. Put on your rubber gloves and use your stain cloth to stain one side of your wood tray, being sure to apply the stain in the direction of the wood grain. Wipe off any excess stain and allow it to dry according to the package instructions. Once the stain is dry, repeat on the other side of the wood tray until it is completely stained and dry, according to package instructions.

2. Use a ruler to find the center of your lazy Susan. Then use your screw gun and wood screws to attach the lazy Susan hardware to the bottom of your wood at the center point.

3. Use your screw gun and wood screws and attach the strap iron along the edge of your wood circle. Add a screw in every other hole, pulling the strap iron tight as you move along. When you reach the end, fold over the edge and attach your last screw.

4. Use your screw gun to attach one handle on each side of the top of your lazy Susan.

DECOUPAGED DRINK COOLER

No matter what type of beverages you serve, from the adult kind to juice boxes, guests seem to linger around the drink table. Of course, everyone always enjoys their drinks chilled, but you don't have to buy a generic cooler to keep your drinks icy cold. Instead, bring a little bit of style and fun to your drink table with this Decoupaged Drink Cooler! Not only does it look cute, but it is easy for your guests to pick out and grab their drink of choice. ▶

Materials

- Scissors
- 3/4 yard of fabric of your choice
  (Note: It is best to choose a fabric that does not have a pattern that only goes in one specific direction.)

- Galvanized bucket (an oval shape seems to work best for this project; I used a container that was 21" × 12" × 8")
- 1" foam paintbrush
- Decoupage medium of your choice (I used Mod Podge)

1. Use your scissors and cut your fabric into two pieces, each able to cover half of the bucket plus a little overlap.

2. You will be working on one side of the outside of your bucket at a time. Use your paintbrush to cover one side of your bucket with your decoupage medium.

3. Using a finished edge, take one of your fabric pieces and line up the top of the fabric with the top lip of the bucket and smooth it in place. Leave your sides loose and pull the bottom section underneath with about 2" of extra fabric, then pull the fabric tight and smooth it out across all areas of the side.

4. Turn your bucket upside down and use your scissors to trim off the extra fabric from the bottom of the bucket. Add additional decoupage medium and push the cut edges down tight.

5. Turn the bucket on its side one more time and press and smooth the fabric to ensure that the whole area is smooth.

6. Use your paintbrush and cover the whole section of fabric with a coat of decoupage medium, then let it dry according to package instructions.

7. Repeat the whole process on the other side.

8. Turn your bucket on its side and trim and fold the fabric to fit around the handles. Fold over the edge of one side and lay it over the other side to leave a finished seam. Cover the whole area in your decoupage medium.

9. Apply two more coats of decoupage medium to the entire bucket, letting it dry in between coats according to the directions on the bottle.

TIPS & RECOMMENDATIONS

When applying coats of decoupage medium over the top of the fabric, the best way to get a smooth and fully covered finish is to do the final smoothing with your hands. Don't be afraid to get a little dirty to get it all smoothed out. Your hands will wash up easily with soap and water.

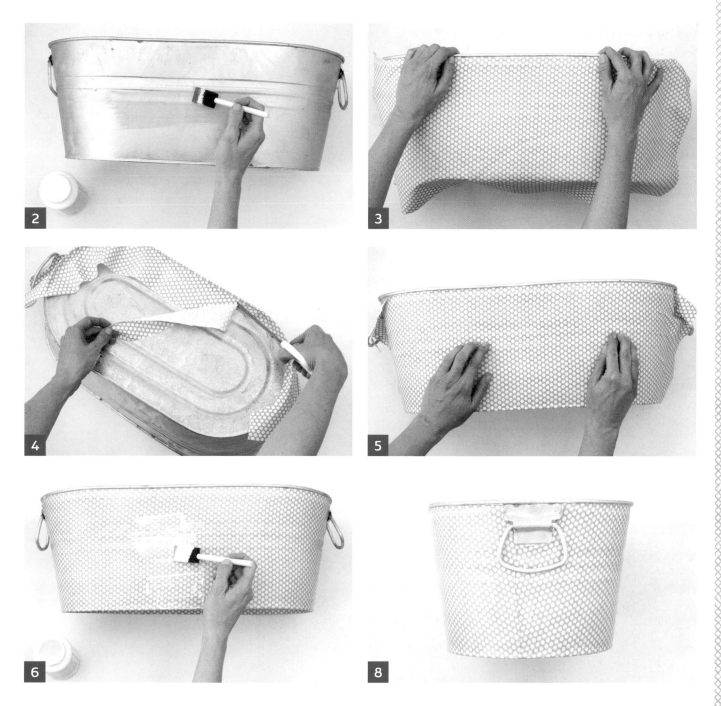

GALVANIZED PEDESTAL

You have to love a DIY that requires no tools and can be done in minutes. This Galvanized Pedestal definitely falls into the "it doesn't get any easier than this" category. This project isn't about the step-by-step process. Instead, it is about looking at things in a different way. By simply turning a bucket upside down and pairing it with a pie plate, you have a whole new piece to use when entertaining or decorating. ▶

Materials

- Heavy-duty craft glue appropriate for metal
- Small galvanized bucket with no handles (if there are handles, remove them with a pair of pliers; the bucket I used is 4" × 4")
- Metal pie plate (the one I used has a 9½" diameter)

1

2

1. Apply glue to the outer edge of the bottom side of the bucket.

2. Center your pie plate on top of the bucket and hold it in place according to package instructions.

3. Then, set aside and allow the glue to dry according to package instructions.

BAR CART

I really don't like to pick favorites, but I absolutely love this project for so many reasons. First, I love the contrast of the wood with the galvanized back. Second, I love that it can be styled out with vintage brass to create another layer of contrast. Third, as great as this works on casters, it would also be beautiful attached right to a wall. Fourth, if a bar cart is not your thing, this piece could be used for so many things: a bookcase, a display case, an extra kitchen storage unit, and even a craft cabinet. This project does require some power tools, but if that is not your thing, you could have the wood cut at the hardware store. This is a beautiful DIY project that anyone can take on with great results. ▸

Materials

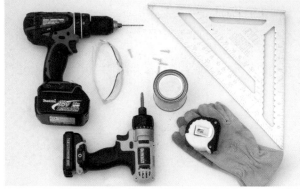

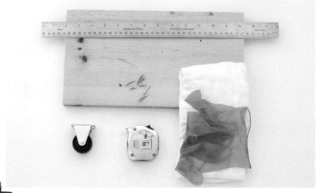

- 2 wood boards for the sides of the cart (I used 36" × 7" × 1" pieces of pine lumber)
- 4 wood boards for the shelves (I used 22³/8" × 7" × 1" pieces of wood)
- Tape measure
- Pencil
- Chop saw (if cutting the boards yourself)
- Square
- Work gloves
- Eye protection
- Stain cloth
- Wood stain
- 24" × 36" piece of sheet metal
- Drill
- Screw gun
- 40 (³/4") wood screws
- Finishing nail gun (optional)
- 24 finishing nails (optional)
- Approximately 28 (³/4") sheet metal screws
- Straightedge
- 4 (2") hooks and plate-mount casters (optional)

1. Finalize the measurements of your cart, buy enough wood at your local lumber or home-improvement store, and if needed have them cut your wood to the sizes of your sides and shelves.

2. If you didn't get your wood cut to size, measure out the sides and shelves on your wood and make your cuts using a chop saw. Your measurements are based on the size of your metal backing, which is 24" × 36". Use a square to ensure your edges are straight and square. Be sure to wear your work gloves and eye protection while operating the chop saw. ▶

3. Put on your rubber gloves and use your stain cloth to stain all sides of your wood (it is not necessary to stain the underside of the bottom), being sure to apply the stain in the direction of the wood grain. Wipe off any excess stain and allow it to dry according to the package instructions.

4. Lay your sheet metal on a worktable and line up your top, bottom, and side pieces of wood by setting the top and bottom pieces inside the side pieces, creating a 90-degree butt joint.

5. Use your drill to drill pilot holes and then use your screw gun to attach screws to connect the joints. Repeat for each of the four corners. For each corner joint, use three screws, one at each side of the sides and one in the center where the boards meet.

6. Determine where you want to place your middle shelves and use your drill to drill pilot holes at the front edges where the middle shelves meet the sides; then use your screw gun and screws to attach the front edges on each side. Use a square to line up the back edges to ensure that your shelf is straight and attach by drilling pilot holes and then connecting with your screw gun and screws. In steps five and six, if you prefer to not use screws, you can also attach the framework together using a finishing nail gun and finishing nails.

7. Place your cabinet face down on your work surface and lay your sheet metal across the back; line up all of the corners. Use sheet metal screws and your screw gun and attach the sheet metal to the edges of your cabinet. Use your square and a straightedge to figure out where your middle shelves are, then mark this spot across the back with a pencil and attach the sheet metal to the back of the middle shelves with sheet metal screws.

TIPS & RECOMMENDATIONS

Customize your look even more by adding hooks or a bottle opener to the sides and casters to the bottom. Also, know that the depth of my wood is 7"; however, that is completely flexible and based on how you want to use the project. All other measurements are based on matching the piece of sheet metal without having to do any metal cuts. My wood is also 1" thick. If you use a different thickness of wood, you have to adjust your measurements accordingly.

Chapter 7

RUSTIC METAL DECORATIVE ACCENTS

I have always loved to decorate my home, even my first apartment. My budget may have required that my ugly couches be covered in sheets, but there were always pretty accents to serve as a distraction. While the previous chapters have covered projects that serve a specific purpose—wall art, lighting, storage, planters, and entertaining—this chapter focuses on projects that are meant just for decorating. Almost every room in my house has some type of galvanized accent that adds a little bit of character and comfort. I love when a project can be used in the home year-round and changed up just a bit for holidays or seasons. Here you'll find tags that can be customized to tie on a gift year-round or hung on a tree at the holidays, along with two types of wreaths that can be used all year and updated for the holidays with a few extra touches, and more! Enjoy!

GALVANIZED LEAF WREATH

This Galvanized Leaf Wreath lived in my head for a long time before I decided to just sit down and figure it out. I love how it takes on the appearance of leaves in nature, like a magnolia leaf, but pairs this natural element with the texture of galvanized metal. ▸

Materials

- Pencil
- Section of galvanized sheet metal (I used about one-third of a 24" × 36" piece, but smaller sizes can be found in hardware stores)
- Work gloves
- Metal snips
- Metal file
- Utility knife
- Straightedge
- 12" MDF wreath form
- Heavy-duty, quick-drying craft glue appropriate for metal
- 10" of ribbon or twine (optional)

1. Use your pencil to draw a leaf shape on your sheet metal. My wreath has sixty-six leaves. I drew a group of about ten leaves at a time and then cut them. Then, I would start again doing about ten leaves at a time. They don't have to be perfect or all the same size. Wear your work gloves while working with the metal and metal leaves. Use your metal snips to cut each leaf out.

2. File the edges of your leaves with a metal file until the edges are smooth.

3. Use your utility knife and your straightedge to score a line down the center of each of your leaves.

4. Use your utility knife to score several lines out from the centerline to create a leaf pattern.

5. Fold each leaf slightly inward and flatten the bottom edge so it will sit better on your wreath form.

6. Attach your leaves to your wreath form one at a time with your craft glue. I generally fanned out three leaves together in a section before moving on to the next section. Place the grouping of three leaves that are fanned out, let them set, then work on the next section by slightly overlapping this section over the previous one. You want to cover the bottom edges of your leaves with the next grouping. It is important to use fast-drying glue so that each leaf holds in place before moving onto the next one. Depending on your glue, each leaf will take about 30 seconds to set enough to move on to the next leaf.

7. Continue adding leaves until you make your way all the way around the wreath. You can thread a 10" section of ribbon or twine around the form of the wreath, tie a knot, and use it to hang the wreath as desired.

TIPS & RECOMMENDATIONS

For year-round use, thread a white ribbon through the wreath form to hang your wreath. Change the color of the ribbon or add a textured fabric like burlap to update it for the seasons and holidays.

END CAP WREATH

From the time I first found galvanized stove end caps at the hardware store, they have made their way into many of my projects. It only seemed fitting that they become a wreath as well. I love that this wreath is beautiful on its own but can filled with so many different types of items and used almost like a curio display. I dressed it out here for summer with shells, coral, and sea glass, but it could be updated and changed out for each holiday or season with ease. ▸

Materials

- · 10" of twine
- · 18" MDF wreath form
- · Heavy-duty craft glue appropriate for metal
- · 9 (3") stove end caps
- · 5 (4") stove end caps
- · Filler items of your choice

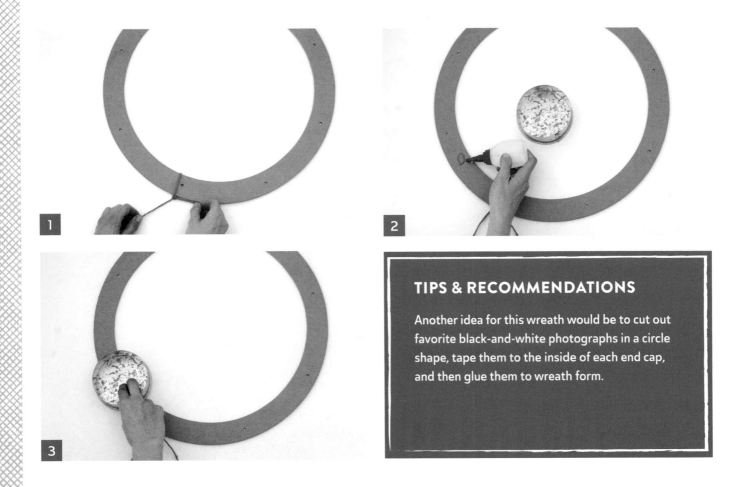

TIPS & RECOMMENDATIONS

Another idea for this wreath would be to cut out favorite black-and-white photographs in a circle shape, tape them to the inside of each end cap, and then glue them to wreath form.

1. Tie the twine onto your wreath form to hang your wreath with when it is complete.

2. Apply glue to your wreath form and attach your first end cap.

3. Add the end caps one at a time in a random order, adding glue to the wreath form before attaching each one; then add your filler items and enjoy!

METAL GIFT TAGS/ORNAMENTS

Over the years I have found galvanized tags and ornaments in stores, but they were never quite right. I either didn't like that they were painted or they weren't the shape that I wanted. Finally I learned how to cut galvanized sheet metal into shapes, which is actually a lot less difficult than I expected. Once I got over that hurdle, it just became about figuring out how to get the shape that I wanted, which turned out to be the easiest idea of all: a cookie cutter. ▸

Materials

- Cookie cutter in your shape of choice (I recommend not using a shape with too many small angles and details)
- Section of galvanized sheet metal
- Pencil
- Metal snips
- Work gloves
- Metal file
- Drill
- 8" of twine per tag

1. Place your cookie cutter on your sheet metal and trace the shape with a pencil.

2. Use your metal snips to cut out your shape. Be sure to wear work gloves while working with the sheet metal as the edges will be sharp.

3. Use your metal file to smooth all of your edges. Take your time with this step to make sure all the edges are smooth.

4. Use your drill to drill a small hole at the top of your tag.

5. Thread a piece of twine through the hole and tie a knot. Hang it on a gift or use it as an ornament.

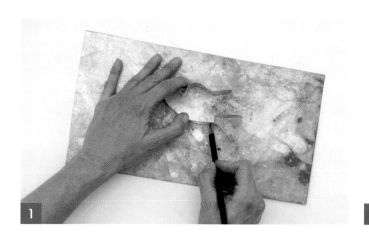

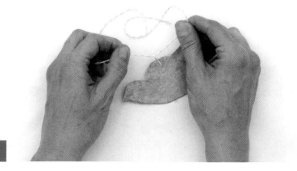

BUCKET SNOWMAN

When the days are gray and filled with snow, it can be hard to find the motivation to head out to a cold workshop and work on a DIY project. This Bucket Snowman is a simple project that brings a little bit of fun to a winter day with no workshop involved. Or, if you have a good sense of humor, this project is a way to bring a snowman into a warm and sunny day.

Materials

- 2 large and similarly sized galvanized buckets (the largest one I used was 24" at the opening)
- Scrap wood (optional)
- 2 medium and similarly sized galvanized buckets
- 2 branches
- Glue gun
- 1 maple syrup bucket (12" × 8") or small bucket
- 2 large buttons
- 10 small buttons
- Carrot
- Hat
- Scarf

1. Place your largest bucket right-side up on the ground and set your second large bucket upside down on top of it. If they don't fit together perfectly, add a piece of scrap wood inside the base bucket to support the next one. ▶

2. Repeat the same process with your medium-sized buckets, but tuck branches in between the buckets for arms. Then stack them on top of the large buckets.

3. Step inside and use a glue gun to adhere your buttons for eyes and a mouth and a carrot for the nose on your smallest bucket.

4. Set your bucket with the face on top of the stack, add a hat, and wrap a scarf around the neck.

BUCKET TREE

I have friends who fill their homes with up to ten trees around the holidays. While I don't go that far, I do love to add a few trees and make them unique. Since there aren't any rules that say trees have to have needles and be green, why not make a galvanized tree? ▶

Materials

- 7 galvanized tubs and buckets in graduated sizes
- About 2 cups of Epsom salts
- 1 quart-size Mason jar
- Votive candle
- Galvanized feed scoop
- 3–5 small pieces of greenery (you can use real or faux)
- Roll of wired ribbon

1. Place your largest tub with the opening facing up where you want to build your tree.

2. Turn your next-largest tub upside down and set it on top of the bottom tub.

3. Stack the remaining buckets in size order until you have all seven stacked.

4. Add Epsom salts to your Mason jar and place your candle inside.

5. Place your Mason jar inside your feed scoop and place it on the top of the stack. Add greenery.

6. Tuck the end of your ribbon under the feed scoop and wrap around the tree until you reach the bottom. Tuck the end behind your tree.

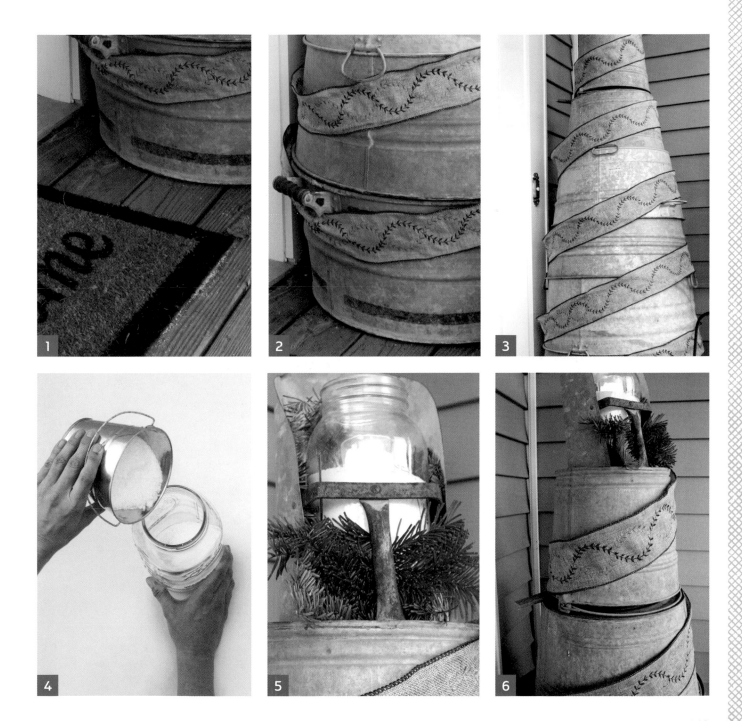

ADVENT TREE

Every year I plan to make an Advent calendar, and before I know it, it is already December 5 and too late to get started. This Advent calendar, besides being adorably cute, will take all that pressure away because it can be used year after year. You simply need to add new treasures to each bucket each year. Keep in mind that Advent calendars don't have to have candy or gifts. A note or a reminder of why someone is loved is just as valuable. ▸

Materials

- 25 galvanized buckets (I used buckets with a 2½" opening)
- Sheet of plywood (my finished tree is 29" high and 20" at its widest point)
- Straightedge
- Pencil

- Angle-measuring tool
- Work gloves
- Jigsaw
- Electric sander
- 1" foam paintbrush

- Small container of white craft paint
- Screw gun
- 25 sheet metal screws
- Scrapbook number stickers (you'll need numbers 1–25)

1. Lay out your buckets in a triangular tree-shape pattern on your plywood and determine the spacing you want. To get twenty-five buckets in a tree shape, starting from the bottom, use six buckets, then five, then four spread out, then four tighter together, then three, then two, and end with one. Mark the length of the bottom of the triangle and draw a line with your straightedge and pencil from one bottom corner to the top point.

2. Next, measure the angle with an angle-measuring tool. (Mine was 70 degrees.)

3. Measure out the same angle on the other side.

4. Draw the line of the triangle for the second side, meeting the first line at the top to make your triangle.

5. Put on your work gloves and use your jigsaw to cut out the shape. ▶

6. Keep your work gloves on and use your power sander to sand the front surface area and the edges of the triangle until they are smooth, then paint your triangle white and allow to dry to the touch according to package instructions.

7. Line up the bottom row of your buckets and attach each one to the plywood at the top of the bucket with a sheet metal screw and your screw gun.

8. Continue with each row until you reach the top and all twenty-five are attached.

9. Number each bucket, starting from the top, with scrapbook number stickers from 1–25. Add your desired gifts and decorations.

8

TIPS & RECOMMENDATIONS

I made my version on a small scale with small buckets; however, the same steps could be used to make a larger version with larger buckets.

FINAL THOUGHTS

When I started the *Finding Home* blog in 2004, I never dreamed it would be what it is today. Finding Home is now a family business with a blog and an online shop where we sell our own line of beautifully handcrafted and delicious maple syrup. It has been an incredible journey so far and I have been thankful for every step—including the hard ones.

Imagine my delight when my journey led to writing this book. I have learned so much in this process that I am so very thankful for. When I first named my blog and then our company, it was out of a desire to find a sense of home in a restless time in our lives. I have always wanted to share ideas and inspiration to help other people make their homes the places where they feel most like themselves. One of the greatest compliments you can pay me is that you are comfortable and relaxed in my home. If this book helps, in even a small way, make other people's homes a place where they are a little bit more comfortable, then I am even more thankful. That would make the work and the effort of this book all worth it.

Thank you for reading and wishing you, as always, a day filled with grace.

Appendix

U.S./METRIC CONVERSION CHART

LENGTH CONVERSIONS	
U.S. Length Measure	**Metric Equivalent**
¼ inch	0.6 centimeters
½ inch	1.2 centimeters
¾ inch	1.9 centimeters
1 inch	2.5 centimeters
1½ inches	3.8 centimeters
1 foot	0.3 meters
1 yard	0.9 meters

INDEX

ABOUT THE AUTHOR

Laura Putnam, based in the Hudson Valley of New York with her husband and two teenage daughters, is the author behind the blog *Finding Home* (*www.findinghomefarms.com*), where she happily shares decorating ideas and DIY projects. Now it is a family affair and she has joined forces with her husband, Dana. They are going for the big dream, making a life and a living doing what they love best—crafting maple syrup and creating a welcoming home. They have built a sugarhouse and an online store so they can share these great passions with you.

Laura has long believed that your home should be where you are most comfortable and a reflection of yourself and your family; she has spent more than a decade helping others create welcoming homes for their families. Now this blog is where she shares her best ideas, inspiration, recipes, and DIY projects to help you create your own dream home and comfort zones. She is somewhat obsessed with galvanized-metal-anything, has never met an old door or vintage toolbox she didn't want to get into a committed relationship with, and has been known to be an incredible klutz, never seeming to have full control of her limbs. And one key point: she is crazy in love with her family and so incredibly grateful for them.

Laura's work has been featured on Apartment Therapy, BHG.com, and CountryLiving.com, and in *Country Woman*, *Better Homes and Gardens Christmas Crafts*, *Make It Yourself*, and *Willow and Sage*.

NOTES